Praise for *Wild Women, Wild Voices*

"In her fourth book, *Wild Women, Wild Voices*, master teacher Judy Reeves's fortifying, fascinating, liberating exercises reach down to the place where the deep howl resides. Writers and nonwriters alike will find energy and passion as they reawaken the wild self."
— Janet Fitch, author of *White Oleander* and *Paint It Black*

"Judy Reeves's books are as wildly wonderful as they come — a must-have for every writer and teacher. Hers are the first I reach for when I write. With the addition of *Wild Women, Wild Voices*, she invites writers at every level to banish shame and cast off their posing gowns. Write on, friends — you've got the best of guides in Judy Reeves."
— Gwendolen Gross, author of *When She Was Gone*

"Judy Reeves has put together a rich, wonderful brew of ideas, quotes, and exercises to unleash the wild writer within you."
— Barbara Abercrombie, author of
A Year of Writing Dangerously and *Kicking In the Wall*

"In *Wild Women, Wild Voices*, Judy Reeves exhorts us to remember the joys and sorrows of our girlhoods; challenges us to examine our relationships with our bodies, our homes, our families, our friends; and invites us to rediscover our inner wildness. Bringing together diverse voices from years of her Wild Women writing workshops, Reeves leads us into a journey toward accessing our most authentic selves, remembering rites of passage, lost dreams, and forgotten selves. With writing prompts, as well as excerpts from beloved writers, this is a book for every woman — whether she writes formally or not — who longs to find her way back to her untamed, creative roots."
— Midge Raymond, author of
Forgetting English and *Everyday Writing*

"Judy Reeves's help in writing as a path to authenticity is beautifully focused, movingly wise, and truly from women's deepest experiences. You feel her there with you on every page of her book, sharing her knowledge and personal journey in the service of guiding you gently to acknowledge your Wild Woman self and free your voice."
— Sheila Bender, WritingItReal.com

"This book will help both novice and experienced writers stare down their fears and inhibitions, embrace their 'wild' voice, and write with exhilarating authenticity."

— Laurel Corona, author of
The Four Seasons and *The Mapmaker's Daughter*

"Wild Women, we've been waiting for this book. Now, at last, Judy Reeves validates all our longings and guides us toward their fulfillment. While reading *Wild Women, Wild Voices*, we follow the quiet hum of our authentic selves all the way to full orchestration. This is a book to buy, tuck under your arm, and head out toward life with, expressing your true self along the way."

— Tina Welling, author of *Writing Wild*

Praise for Judy Reeves's *A Writer's Book of Days*

"*A Writer's Book of Days* is the best sort of writer's book: You feel like writing as you read it! It is a spring-fed fountain of inspiration for the writers in us all. This book dances around the imagination and makes you take out your pens and journal to play."

— SARK, author/artist of *Succulent Wild Woman*
and *Glad No Matter What*

"Judy Reeves is a writer who lives in her writing, who lives to write. Her passion and dedication to other writers, her community, and her own process are an inspiration for all of us."

— Tom Spanbauer, author of *Faraway Places*
and *The Man Who Fell in Love with the Moon*

"A delightful mix of commonsense and inspiration, *A Writer's Book of Days* provides the ongoing voice of the teacher, coach, friend, and support group available on call. I suggest this book to every writing seminar graduate — a way to take the experience home and carry on."

— Christina Baldwin, author of *Storycatcher*,
The Seven Whispers, *Life's Companion*, and *The Circle Way*

WILD WOMEN, WILD VOICES

Also by Judy Reeves

A Creative Writer's Kit

A Writer's Book of Days

The Writer's Retreat Kit

Writing Alone, Writing Together

WILD WOMEN, WILD VOICES

Writing from Your Authentic Wildness

JUDY REEVES

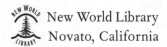

New World Library
Novato, California

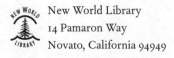
New World Library
14 Pamaron Way
Novato, California 94949

Text design by Tona Pearce Myers

Library of Congress Cataloging-in-Publication Data
Reeves, Judy, date.
Wild women, wild voices : writing from your authentic wildness / Judy Reeves.
    pages   cm
ISBN 978-1-60868-295-9 (paperback) — ISBN 978-1-60868-296-6 (ebook)
1. Authorship—Miscellanea. 2. Creative writing—Miscellanea. 3. Women—Authorship. I. Title.
PN165.R38 2015
808.02—dc23   2014045552

First printing, April 2015
ISBN 978-1-60868-295-9
Printed in Canada on 100% postconsumer-waste recycled paper

New World Library is proud to be a Gold Certified Environmentally Responsible Publisher. Publisher certification awarded by Green Press Initiative. www.greenpressinitiative.org

10   9   8   7   6   5   4   3   2   1

For my mother, Evelyn Maxine Sandusky Gray

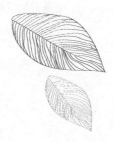

CONTENTS

INTRODUCTION

A little more than two decades ago, I received a copy of Clarissa Pinkola Estés's book *Women Who Run with the Wolves*. In the introduction I read, "No matter by which culture a woman is influenced she understands the words wild and woman, intuitively." Something about the way those two words — *wild* and *woman* — were placed alongside each other set up a commotion inside me, a response to a longing I couldn't name. "When a woman hears those words," Estés continued, "an old, old memory is stirred and brought back to life."

My husband had died a few years earlier, and I'd recently returned from a journey in which I'd effectively exiled myself to traveling the world solo, with one suitcase and no set itinerary. Call it a quest or a soul search; it was one of those times of psychic if not physical upheaval that most of us experience at some time in our lives. I was easy prey for seduction by such an old, old memory.

At the time, I'd taken up with a circle of women who were studying the old religions and folkways and creating celebrations to honor the seasonal cycles of the earth — the solstices and equinoxes. While it was not exactly primal, there was in our work a deep and intuitive connection to the wild feminine. And though we didn't actually break any laws, we did leave a few muddy footprints on some rules — spoken, written, and implied — of what the present culture defines as acceptable.

1

At each of our meetings we set aside a generous amount of time for writing in our journals or notebooks. We'd respond to exercises or prompts that invited explorations into our experiences, our memories, our stories. We'd write in silence and then, if we wanted, read aloud what we'd written. There was no feedback on the writing, but you could feel in the room how one woman's words affected the whole. A web, strong and silky as a spider's, connected us. And though I've been a lifelong daily journaler, it was the prompts, questions, and explorations initiated by our work that took me into the deep waters of memory and experience, where I knew how to swim as if by instinct and swore I could breathe underwater. I wrote with a passion I had only rarely experienced, though I've been writing since I was a child. Words poured from my pen onto the page in a language I didn't know I could speak. There was no struggle, no questioning, no doubting — just this unrestrained, ferocious, sometimes funny, always passionate wild voice. And it wasn't just me. Other women in the group found themselves writing with this same freedom and depth, each in her unique and powerful voice.

In these gatherings I discovered something profoundly empowering — and not only empowering, but holy. We weren't reciting prayers or singing songs taught to us in some long-ago Sunday school; we were making our own joyful noise. We were flinging off our shoes and dancing our own dances. And laughing! Until you've been in a roomful of women in which that bawdy laughter has been unleashed, you have not heard the howl of a pack of Wild Women. And if you are a woman and you've read this far, you know the open-mouthed, hold-your-sides, cross-your-legs-or-you'll-pee kind of laughter I'm talking about.

That howl of raucous laughter wasn't the only sound made during our times together, or during any of the times I've been in a collective of renegade women who felt safe enough to voice their anger, name their regrets, and weep for their losses.

But it's not only tears and laughter, impulses and memories, that link us to our authentic wildness. By nature we are creative. Creativity flows through us like the blood in our veins. In our natural state, we are writers, dancers, singers, poets, and makers of art, even though in our daily lives we may not practice our art or even acknowledge this part of ourselves. Still, our hands intuitively know the shape of a bowl; our fingers naturally curve around a pen or brush. We sing when we're alone in the car or the shower and dance by ourselves when we hear a certain song.

We know many things: why spiders like dark places, why moths are drawn to the light; we know the urging of blossom to break open every spring. Given a clear night and a blanket spread on the summer grass, we can translate the midnight language of the stars. We understand the necessity of sex, the order of death, the beauty of mourning.

These are intuitive knowings that we sometimes forget, but they reside just beneath the surface of our daily lives and come alive in our nightdreams. Try as culture, politics, religion, or families might to eradicate it, this knowledge of our innermost Self — intuitive and rich and wild — is always with us. We may have forgotten how to express it or we might stutter when we try, but the deep song of our authentic voice still resonates within.

This is the ongoing and important work of Wild Women: to give voice to an authentic expression of thoughts and feelings that are often ignored or belittled or set aside for when we can finally claim some time for ourselves. To remember our stories and share them with others or keep them, safe and sacred, within the private pages of our journals. To value our creative nature and respond to its urgings.

After a few years our women's group disbanded, but our time together and the connection I experienced to a creative and fierce feminine spirit hummed inside me. I missed the dedicated time of what I knew to be soul work, and I missed the sound of my untamed, wild voice. I'd come to recognize a certain yearning that arose in me as regularly as the cycles of the moon. You may have experienced symptoms of this yourself, standing in front of the mirror unable to recognize your own face, wandering the burgeoning aisles of a store and finding nothing you want to buy. Or just the opposite: loading up your cart and discovering later that none of what you brought home satisfies you. Maybe you have shed those unexpected tears or felt that sudden anger or the loneliness that ambushes you when you're in a crowd. Dreamed up words that cannot find their way to the page.

It was this longing that led me to form the Wild Women writing workshop. Within these weekly gatherings of creative women I found I wasn't the only one who responded to the words *wild* and *woman*. We were a mélange of artists and teachers, lawyers and home-care workers, masseuses and physical therapists, businesswomen and stay-at-home moms, retired women and women just entering their adult lives. Some of us were writers by career or by life choice, others of us kept journals or were drawn to writing as a mode of expression but weren't regular practitioners. What we had in common was an itching curiosity, a desire we might not have been able to put a name to, and an instinctual response to the coupled words *wild* and *woman*.

As happened to me in the women's circle and in any number of gatherings since — and ultimately in the privacy of my own writing space — *wild voice* was what was spoken in these groups.

As its name implies, wild voice is untamed and unbounded and holds the possibility of great beauty. It goes deep, like roots; it sings because it can. It is not domesticated or restrained. Wild voice can be dangerous; it can be outrageous. It is passionate, exuberant, and eager for life. It is turbulent and stormy, often arriving as unexpectedly as a summer squall. It can also appear as tranquil as an autumn breeze or a lazy river — but just try to capture either of these in a bottle and put them on a shelf.

Language erupts spontaneously with wild voice. The bird emerges from a cracked-open egg, the butterfly escapes from the chrysalis, fire explodes from the creosote bush. Wild voice is what gives you the sentence or phrase that seems to come out of nowhere. It is what wants to be expressed. When wild voice speaks, we pay attention. It tells you what matters and what you intuitively know.

The material in this book was drawn from the Wild Women writing workshops. Thirteen chapters invite exploration into all the varied aspects of our lives, times we lived our wildish nature and times we allowed ourselves to be domesticated. The path is not chronological, beginning with birth and ending with old age. Instead, we wander a road less traveled, looking at ourselves as girls and our initiation into womanhood, remembering and acknowledging ourselves as artists and creators and as adventurous travelers of inner and outer landscapes. Chapters are devoted to our relationship with our bodies; to psychic as well as physical geography; to the meaning of home; to family and who we are as daughter, sister, mother; to loves and lovers; to friendship with other women. We examine our dreams — both by day and by night — and we create our own myths and structure our own stories. Through accessing our wild voice, we see how our lives have been influenced by intuition and the role synchronicity may have played. We'll touch the dark edges of our shadow selves, exploring how this aspect is related to our creativity and our renegade nature. We give death its time as well.

Wild Women, Wild Voices is constructed as a guide to help you access memories and experiences, beliefs and imaginings, and write them from deep, authentic wildness. In our Wild Women writing workshops, this work was the territory where discoveries were made and memories resurrected and recounted in a new way. Writing explorations took participants deep into the vein of their own wisdom, where secret doors fell open and intuition connected seemingly disparate dots. These explorations have been added to and expanded in the book. Also included in each of the chapters are evocative poems and excerpts of stories and essays written by women in the groups as well as by other writers, some whose names you might recognize and others whom you may meet for the first time.

This book is an invitation for you to write your stories. We won't be talking about plot or character development or theme. Instead, each chapter will present a series of explorations that summon you to follow your pen on a narrative journey into memory and experience, with wild voice as storyteller.

Just as with other practices that take us deeper into our intuitive nature — meditation, yoga, qigong — we reap the greatest benefit from our work if we practice it daily. The first chapter describes some tools and practices meant to aid you in your journey. They will call forth from you a commitment of time set aside and honored, a willingness to trust the process, an open mind and heart, and definitely a sense of humor. This is important work, giving time and expression to your deep and authentic nature and acknowledging your Wild Woman and giving her voice.

Recently, I asked some women from past Wild Women writing workshops, and others whom I identified as "wild" (was it the bits of leaves and twigs still caught their hair?), what the words *wild* and *woman* conjured for them.

They used words such as *free* and *unpredictable*, *strong* and *uncontrollable*, *natural* and *fierce*, *deep dreaming* and *farsighted*. "It's a part of me that knew what was true before I learned words to describe it," said Helen, one of the participants. *Boundlessness*, the women said, *energy* and *creativity*, *joy* and *freedom. Risk taking, curious, brave, wise, feral,* and *extraordinary in her splendid glorious way of being.*

Maybe you would use some of the same words. Or others of your own conjuring. The thing is, something has drawn you to this work. For each of us, this catalyst is different: maybe it was the sound of the wind in the trees, a gathering of birds, a line in a poem. A nightdream in which a voice spoke to you, expressing an inner urging that your life was "too much" or "not enough." Or perhaps it was simply a longing, a yearning, a restlessness with no name that was calling you to listen, and to speak in the voice of your wild and authentic self.

1 MAPS FOR THE JOURNEY

Once upon a time...
Long ago and far away...
In a land that never was and a time that could never be...
I remember...

Ever since human beings invented language, these words, or words like them, have signaled the approach of a story. We have always been story-telling creatures. From the beginning, myths, folktales, and fairy tales have told of human flaws and frailties, of meeting and overcoming threats and challenges, and of human transformation and redemption. You and I tell stories of our daily lives. We can't help ourselves. We meet a friend in the grocery store and stand beside the bananas for fifteen minutes, telling stories. Our children come home from school and say, "Guess what happened?" Ask someone, "How was your day?" and prepare to settle in for a tale.

We tell stories to give shape to experiences, to entertain, to process, to grieve, to heal, and to share our perspective on the world. Our stories reside in place, in things, in relationships and events. And, oh, the stories in our families... "The fact is that anybody who has survived childhood has enough information about life to last him the rest of his days," Flannery O'Connor tells us.

By *story*, I mean a narrative rather than a particular structure or format. Telling stories is how we relate a memory and how we identify ourselves. A story can be a few paragraphs describing an incident or experience, it can be the description of a place, or it can be a series of dialogue exchanges. A story can even be a grocery list. It can be six words or six hundred words or six times six hundred words: whatever it takes. One word following another and the one after that until we reach The End.

Responding to the call of your wild voice signals a departure, if even for a brief time, from your ordinary world and an entrance into the world where your wildish nature resides. And like the protagonist in the classic hero's journey who, after many challenges, receives a great gift that he brings home to share with the world, you can return with a gift, too. Your gift will be the stories you discover and relate in your creative, ferocious, and authentic wild voice. How you choose to share your gift — writing for yourself, writing for your friends and family, writing for a wider audience through publication — is up to you. I believe that the world longs for each of us to use our creative gifts, whatever they may be and however they want to be expressed.

You Are Here: Beginning the Journey

During the Wild Women writing workshops, we meet once a week, working our way through the sections of this book. You may want to follow the same schedule — reading the text, responding to the questions, and completing some of the writing explorations to create your own self-guided weekly workshop. You may find, as have others, the questions and explorations so compelling that you'll want to take time to respond to all of them. Though you can certainly do this work alone, you might like to invite other women to join you. (A guide on forming your own *Wild Women, Wild Voices* group can be found in the appendix.) As I've experienced countless times, and maybe you have, too, some powerful mojo happens when women join together to do the deep work of the soul.

Whichever way you choose — a solitary journey or traveling in a pack — you will need a map for the journey. Following are some suggestions that will guide you along the way.

Claim Your Wild Nature

Claiming your wild nature as you set out on the journey is the first step. By saying, "Yes!" to this inner calling, you give voice to your intention, confirming your commitment to your Self. However you make this claim — an affirmation that you say upon waking and that you repeat throughout the day, a ringtone on your phone that serves as a call to prayer, a love note to your wildish self stuck in your wallet — these small, personal expressions will act as declarations of your claim and enable you to take the next step in your journey. So write those two words, *wild* and *woman,* next to each other on a sticky note on your bathroom mirror or write them in a bold shade of lipstick, and repeat them to yourself each morning as you look in the mirror. Recognize and acknowledge the natural wildness in you and your voice, give a wink or a growl, and get on with it.

Set Aside Time

Right about now you may be thinking, "Time? That's what I have least of." But what I've seen happen for more than a few who make the commitment is that once we begin mining our memories; writing our stories; and giving ourselves over to what our minds, bodies, and spirits respond to, as if by magic more time becomes available. Our priorities shift and we find ourselves saying no to distractions that aren't as rich or fulfilling and yes to ourselves and our journey.

Experience shows that we're more likely to keep a date with ourselves if we note the time in a calendar or datebook, especially until we can build a practice that comes as naturally as taking a shower and is as rewarding as having a massage. Telling a supportive friend, especially a friend who will hold you accountable, maybe someone who is taking this journey with you, of your commitment can also help you honor your intention.

Because I mostly teach in the evening, I reserve first thing in the morning for my daily writing practice. When I had a day job that started early in the morning, I'd often take time during my lunch hour and get away from the office. Sometimes I'd camp out in my car with my notebook and pen for ten or twenty minutes of writing solitude. Using your afternoon coffee break, arising an hour earlier in the morning, taking an hour or so away from usual evening distractions: it doesn't matter when you do the work, only that you do it.

Record Your Journey Notes

I have been a journal keeper for as long as I can remember. Once I learned the basics of writing practice, from Natalie Goldberg's seminal book *Writing Down the Bones*, I have been a proponent and a disciple, first doing my own daily writing, then leading writing practice groups, and eventually publishing *A Writer's Book of Days*, based on my experiences as a regular practitioner. More than two decades later, I still write daily in my journal and do writing practice regularly.

In this book I'm calling this daily practice Journey Notes. Writing our observations, reflections, and stories helps us to clarify our thoughts and discover what matters to us. What shows up on the page can reveal understandings about our lives and ourselves that we might never gain otherwise. So often I've heard participants in my writing groups say, when reading back something they've written, "I haven't thought of that in years" or "I've never had that memory before" or "I didn't realize how important that was to me."

Daily writing practice encourages and nurtures wild voice. This is the voice that will come naturally when you give yourself over to the writing, without thought to structure, rules, or audience.

A daily writing practice has many other benefits as well. Writing can put words to feelings and allow us to write through them to the other side. It can be very cathartic. Writing is also a doorway to memories, bringing them into sharper view when we name the details and recall small occasions and incidents.

In her essay "The Site of Memory" Toni Morrison writes about the Mississippi River being straightened in places to make room for houses and livable acreage. "Occasionally the river floods in these places...but in fact it is not flooding; it is remembering. Remembering where it used to be. All water has a perfect memory and is forever trying to get back to where it was. Writers are like that: remembering where we were, what valley we ran through, what the banks were like, the light that was there and the route back to our original place. It is emotional memory — what the nerves and the skin remember as well as how it appeared. And a rush of imagination is our 'flooding.'"

Writing our Journey Notes, we can ask questions and find the answers. Questions, after all, are what lead us into the deeper and often secret places of our inner knowing.

Give your wild voice free and open range as you write. Sometimes, when we're able to get our busy minds out of the way, this daily writing allows us to "take dictation." That is, we write in a language that comes directly from our intuitive knowing — the voice of our wiser self. It is our soul-voice, telling us truths; it is wild voice. In my writing groups, women often shake their heads and say in a voice filled with wonder, "I don't know where that came from." But I know. "It came from you," I tell them.

Thoughts, memories, bits and pieces of story, lines of what might become a poem, fragments of what could have been a dream, bones of something half-known and mostly intuited: all these go into your Journey Notes. Open up. Set the page on fire with your words, or soothe your mad imaginings with the language of your heart. Let your breathing create a rhythm for your hand, and let your hand follow your heart to places wide and deep and free flowing.

Whether you decide on a time-bound or a page-bound practice (fifteen or twenty minutes, two or three pages), I recommend writing by hand, and I'm not the only one. Julia Cameron suggests this as well: "Even the shape of my writing tells me the shape and clarity of my thoughts," she writes. And in an interview with the *Paris Review*, Pablo Neruda said, "The typewriter separated me from a deeper intimacy with poetry, and my hand brought me closer to that intimacy again." Though we may not be writing poetry, writing by hand creates an intimacy with our whole being. It connects us to our senses, our emotions, our bodies, and our breath and allows us access to our deepest knowing.

You don't have to be a "writer" to experience the benefits of this daily practice. Simply putting words on the page, one at a time, without judgment or critique, will coax your wild voice to speak. In our writing practice groups we say, "Don't judge, compare, or analyze the writing, just write." Don't worry about the rules, grammar, or anything else, and don't go back and read what you've written until you're done. Don't worry if you sometimes can't read your own writing. Don't worry that what you thought you were going to write about isn't what appears on the page. What shows up is the story that wanted to be written — who can say why? Don't worry about anything. Embrace the surprises.

Always the teacher, I've included writing tips along the way, and suggestions for nurturing your wild voice. Some of these may be style guidelines you already know, others may help you access details or relate something in a way you haven't considered before. My hope is that these ideas will guide your writing toward more clarity, aliveness, and depth.

Any kind of book — a blank book, a bound journal, or a spiral-bound notebook (do you want to carry yours around in your bag or pocket?) will serve for your Journey Notes. It can be plain or fancy, store bought or homemade, an artist's sketchbook, or blue-lined paper. Maybe you want to use paper that's preprinted or hand decorated with images that inspire and influence your writing. Participants in the Wild Women writing workshops often create an original cover for their notebooks. While some might advise against using expensive journals or hand-crafted paper, saying that all the fancy might inhibit the writing, I say go with what inspires the pen to move and the words to flow. Go with what feels most authentic to you.

Leave Waymarks along the Trail

We women often set aside our alone time to perform the tasks associated with our many and varied roles, yet this aloneness is the very thing we need in order to hush the din of the world enough to hear our soul-voice.

Growing up in a family of four sisters, I often heard my mother plead: "If I could just get a little peace and quiet..." (She also often said, "You girls are driving me crazy!") But my mother, like so many women of her generation, was never able to find the peace and quiet that comes with alone time, and when the last of us sisters finally left home, she was so steeped in domesticity, so timid of anything beyond the realm that had defined her for so long, that she never attempted to step outside its boundaries. Still, in spite of all outward appearances, I don't doubt for a moment that Wild Woman lived inside my mother, just as it does in every woman. As a child, I crawled under the kitchen table often enough during my mother's coffee klatches with her friends to hear the bawdy laughter that marks any gathering of our tribe. I'm certain that all the years of lacking solitude — this distance from her own voice — not only limited my mother's connection to her wild nature but also accounted for her attempts to suppress my wild child instincts.

Solitude is a lovely word, often taken as meaning "loneliness." But really it's just the opposite; it's the kind of aloneness that being complete with our Self allows. May Sarton wrote, "Loneliness is the poverty of self; solitude is richness of self." Creating a ritual for our daily work is one way to find the solitude necessary for a dialogue with our deepest selves.

No matter where I've lived, and my friends will tell you I've lived a lot of places, I have always created a special place where I can go, alone, first thing every morning to read my meditation books and do my daily writing. Others tell me they do the same, though the specific details — a special chair, a desk at the window that overlooks the garden, the garden itself

— may be very different, and they may not call them a ritual. "A cup of tea and back in bed with my notebook" is my friend Jill's routine. Dian escapes to her office, where between seeing clients, she sequesters herself with her writing. Lisa's living room can be shut off completely from the rest of the house, even the dogs, and there she has a chair that is "just for her." In my current apartment I'm a kitchen table writer, though you'll often find me taking my notebook on a mini-retreat to the park or to a café or to the library. It doesn't surprise me anymore that some of the quietest times I've experienced have been when I'm alone at a table in a crowded café.

Create a Space

A few years ago I had the opportunity to see the stunning installation of Judy Chicago's *The Dinner Party* in the Elizabeth A. Sackler Center for Feminist Art at the Brooklyn Museum. Chicago's iconic masterpiece features elaborate handmade place settings for thirty-nine mythical and real-life famous women along a triangular table that measures forty-eight feet on each side. A tiled floor engraved with the names of nine hundred and ninety-nine additional women lies beneath the grand display.

Creating a space for your daily dialogues with yourself is like setting the table for a feast. Yours will most likely not be as flamboyant as Judy Chicago's, but whether it's simple or elaborate, by furnishing it with elements that are meaningful to you, you mark the space as special and the time you spend there as sacred.

I love the title of Rebecca Wells's novel *Little Altars Everywhere*. Creating little altars is something we do naturally; I have them all over my house — at my writing desk, on my bedside table, lining my bookshelves. Maybe for you it's a special stone you found on a walk and brought home and placed just so, or the tiny figure of Quan Yin you discovered in a bookstore that rides along on the dashboard of your car, or the silver heart that lives on your bathroom shelf, along with your collection of sea glass and shells. My friend Anita has a miniature doghouse with Snoopy perched atop the roof — beagles are that special to her. Barbara has a small statue of the Buddha. I do my morning writing in the kitchen, and on the ledge of the window there, I keep an amethyst crystal, still in its natural state. I love the way the sunlight burrows in the rough crevices and sends out flashes of lavender.

When you imbue these items with the power to carry your intention they become charms or totems, their presence inspiring or soothing, reminding you of who you are and what matters to you. In *The Book of Awakening*, Mark Nepo wrote, "Symbols are the living mirrors of the deepest understandings that have no words."

Each chapter in this book includes the suggestion that you add to your altar or writing table something that speaks to you or that represents that chapter's focus. At our Wild Women writing workshops our table held skate keys, stuffed animals, and bird nests during the Wild Child, Wild Girl session; love letters, wedding photos, and red lace lingerie during the Loves and Lovers session; and artwork of all kinds during the Artist/Creator week. While you work with the material in each chapter, your special object can serve as inspiration and will symbolize your desire to communicate with your deepest Self and to speak from your authentic voice.

Light a Candle

At the beginning of each Wild Women writing workshop, as well as of many other retreats and workshops I lead, I traditionally light a candle. If I forget, one of the participants is sure to remind me. They know lighting the candle is a way to symbolize that we are crossing the threshold into a time out of time. I light a candle every morning, too, when I sit down to do my daily meditation reading and journal writing and when I do my writing practice at home or on retreat. Even at the cafés I frequent I light an imaginary candle before I begin writing.

Just as we light candles for holiday dinners or before a long, fragrant soak in the bathtub, lighting a candle as we begin writing is another way to signify we are creating a special time and place. Ambiance yes, but more than that. During our writing, we are reminded that while the candle is lit, we are in a holy place doing holy work, even if what we write feels mundane or veers toward the shadows. It's doing the work that is holy, the process.

Lighting candles is symbolic in other ways, too — fire is one of the four natural elements, along with air, water, and earth, and this reminds us of our deep connection with the natural world. Candles light our way, keep the dark at bay, and create fire for our literary cookstoves. Let the lighting of your candle each day call forth your wildish nature.

Setting Out

And so we begin our journey. In fairy tales and folktales, the heroine is often aided in completing seemingly impossible tasks by a helper, a powerful, magical person or animal. In our own work, we can consider this helper to be our wiser self, our intuition, the spirit of Wild Woman who is with us always. Just as we rely on our senses — sight, smell, taste, touch, hearing — to give us information and enhance our daily lives, our intuitive voice, the sixth sense, can serve as our compass and our guiding light. You can trust this inner voice. It comes from your deep wild nature. Follow its lead.

You may have other helpers along the way as well, such as signs of synchronicity or coincidences — the perfect book that falls from the shelf, a phone call from a friend just when you need some words of encouragement. A message might come in the form of a song, a news report, a poem scrawled on the sidewalk in chalk. Pay attention. When you undertake this journey to give voice to your authentic wildness, the Universe will cooperate with you.

While this journey is a great adventure, committing to it takes courage. The old tales often relate the world as a dangerous place, saying warnings must be heeded or certain costs will be levied. In myths, folktales, and fairy tales, these costs can be drastic — losing feet and hands or being turned into frightful or foolish animals or being transformed into glass or salt or stone. Though we may not realize it, the costs of turning a deaf ear to the inner calling of our wild nature are just as high — the loss of passion, a lack of sensitivity to our natural rhythms, a forgetfulness of our intuitive wisdom that comes from living and speaking authentically.

It takes courage to listen, to act on the messages from our deepest knowing, and to write what wants to be written from this place. But, as the old stories tell us, and this is the most important message, if you have courage, if you persist, if you hold to the truth and remain faithful to your deepest knowing, miracles can happen: you can slay the dragon, receive new understanding, and return home with a great gift.

Are you ready? Let us set out.

2 CLAIMING WILD WOMAN

*No matter by which culture a woman is influenced, she understands
the words wild and woman, intuitively.*

    *When a woman hears those words, an old, old memory is
stirred and brought back to life. The memory is of our absolute,
undeniable, and irrevocable kinship with the wild feminine.*

— Clarissa Pinkola Estés

I t is time. Prepare your space. Bring to your altar (or table
or desk) whatever you have chosen to represent your wildish nature, a tribute to your Wild Woman. Light your candle.
Offer a prayer if you want, or begin by reading a poem or a
quote that speaks of your intention. Maybe you'll want music
for the journey, or to begin with a few moments of meditation.
Now is the time for anything that marks crossing the threshold
from ordinary time to a time set aside for *you*. You have come
to claim your wild self.

    What are the first words you write in your wild voice?

    What is the shape of the letters written in your wild hand?

    What is the sound of your authentic wildness?

    It would not be unusual, right now, for you to sit with pen
in hand, hand poised above notebook, unsure where to begin.
Feeling that each word or sentence you begin to write is the
wrong one. That each thought expressed is not exactly what
you want to say. And so you gaze away, stare into your candle,

look out the window, consider your hands as they hold your pen, notice that fingernail that needs to be filed.

The more you think, the more difficult the actual writing becomes.

This is because Wild Woman doesn't reside in the brain. We can't think her any more than we can think a flower to bloom or lightning to flash. She comes to us naturally, intuitively. To give her voice, we best get out of our own way. She speaks through us, not to us, and not in calculated words but in the language of the soul, the body, our wildish nature that lives below the surface. This voice, your authentic and wild and beautiful voice, doesn't come from thinking but instead comes as a response, sometimes through a vision, as Estés wrote: "Through sights of great beauty…through music, which vibrates the sternum, excites the heart…sometimes a word, a sentence or a poem or a story, is so resonant, so right, it causes us to remember, at least for an instant, what substance we are really made from, and where is our true home." And in this instant, your words form honestly and easily, without strain.

However, getting from here to there isn't always easy. A friend once told me that when she was a young girl she believed that everyone except her could turn off their brain at will, like flipping a switch. "How else could they go to sleep at night?" she wondered. Of course she wasn't far into her adult life when she learned that few of us can simply turn off our minds anytime we want. This is why we need meditation, the ringing of chimes, the song of the prayer bowl, the return to the breath.

Qualities of Wild Woman Nature

We begin our journey by Claiming Wild Woman. This is where we affirm who we are and where we declare our selfhood. It is where we locate the source of our wild song.

But we may have some excavating to do. Perhaps our kinship with the wild feminine has become "ghosty from neglect,
buried by overdomestication, outlawed by the surrounding
culture." And so writing in the authentic wild voice doesn't
come easily. We may need to brush away the dust and cobwebs
that have muffled that voice to a whisper. Your true voice may
be buried beneath ideas of who you think you are supposed to
be, what you think you are supposed to sound like, what you
think you *should* write.

Wild Woman and wild voice are deeply connected; within
one is the other. And so we go to the source to affirm the qualities of our wild self. Here we don't attempt to explain; we
respond in images. Following are some of the images that came
to me as I wrote this section.

Something deep in the body, the color red
Smells earthy
Barefoot, strong, and surefooted
Fierce in love, in caring, in connection
Deep dreaming, farsighted
"Memory thick as mud"
Body knowing, heart singing, love making
The poetry of breathing
Hears ancient echoes. Holy sounds from above and below
Solitude and community in equal measure
Cycles moon shaped, nature connected
Feels blessed by the sunrise, anointed by the moon
Breathes in life, breathes out death

When asked for their response, women expressed Wild
Woman in various ways. She is "wise beyond this reality,"
said my friend Barbara. Karin related some of the qualities as
actions: "Running through the ocean waves at sunset, dancing

around a fire pit at 2:00 AM, riding my bike scary fast with my hair streaming out behind me." Pamela wrote, "Freedom, curiosity, a great capacity for delight and feeling at home in one's skin."

Freedom was a word used frequently by the women in the workshops, as was *creative*. Wild Woman is, by nature, creative. She takes risks and revels in her authenticity. There is something mysterious, even spiritual about her. She is deeply connected with both the Earth and the Universe; she doesn't shy away from her own numinosity. "Sometimes this fierceness deep inside...amazes me," wrote Madaline.

Now it's your turn. As your first act of Claiming Wild Woman, begin by naming your own wild qualities.

EXPLORATION: My Wild Woman Qualities

Writing from images and imagination, make a list of your wild qualities. Remember, keep your pen moving, and don't stop to think of the words; let them come through you. If you want, set a timer to help you with the "not thinking part." Go for two or three minutes. Your images and phrases may surprise you as something like a poem emerges from them.

From these images, create messages to yourself and place them around your workspace to remind you of your wild nature. Stash one in your bathroom vanity, slide one in your desk drawer so that you'll see it when you reach for your paper clips or Scotch tape. I keep some of the words on my altar and change them as one starts to resonate more deeply than the others. As I write this, the word *untamed* in bright magenta letters reminds me of how I want my words to form.

Put sticky notes on your monitor, write tiny messages to keep in your purse — put one in your wallet with your money — write a blank check made out to one of your wild qualities.

Each day in your Journey Notes journal write one aspect of your wild nature and freewrite how you express that quality.

Connecting with Our Wild Nature

For eons men, and sometimes women, too, have made light of "women's intuition." Yet a more powerful, knowing force does not exist. All humans are gifted with this sixth sense — my husband used to talk about the little bell he heard inside, a warning to pay attention. But intuition is strongest in the feminine. For women, especially women who abide in their wild nature, this intuition is a direct link to the soul. Its voice is sure and true. Maybe this very strength, this "right-on-ness," is what has made it the butt of jokes and the object of sarcasm. We all know that laughing at what we fear can take away some of its power. But rather than fearing this inner knowing, as Wild Women we embrace it. We surrender to its guidance. For when we not only listen but also rely on our intuition, we know what we need, what is good for us, and what we hunger for. When we are at one with our wild and true nature, we trust ourselves. We are surefooted.

"I feel my most authentic self when I listen to my inner voice," said Ellen. "Over the years I have realized it speaks truth and when I listen to its guidance, I am almost always making a good decision — be it with relationships or experiences."

It didn't surprise me when many women, speaking about when they felt their most authentic, mentioned writing, making art, creating through craft, acting, dancing without inhibition. "I have felt my most authentic self when I'm following my inner muse," said Anitra. "Riffing on a tune, writing, making art, bodysurfing the waves, bodysurfing some body..."

Donna wrote about her experience as a writer: "It's a strange moment in time when the writing is cooking — exhilarating and unnerving at the same time. This kind of connection, of being plugged in, has a physical manifestation. Afterward, I may feel drained, but it's a good kind of tired, the fatigue of having created something that I know could only have come from me."

Many of us, as we toil away at our day jobs inside office complexes or our home offices, at hospitals or in schoolrooms, or any of the other enclosed, often concrete, sometimes windowless structures, miss our connection with nature. It may be in nature that we most feel that ages-old call of the wild.

"I work as a database administrator for a biotech company," said Karin. "The computers get inside my brain, change the way I think and leave me functioning in a robotic state, alienated from my authentic self. In nature, far away from the call of humans, I become Artemis, Wild Woman and virgin, listening to the wisdom of the Universe whispering in my heart."

"I didn't grow up with woods and wild land around me, and so I didn't realize how much I loved it until I discovered it in the Pacific Northwest," Midge wrote from her home in Oregon. "I now feel most at home out in nature."

When we listen to our internal calling, when we trust it enough to follow, sometimes magic happens. "Moths follow me everywhere, day and night, even in the winter when there shouldn't be moths. I commune with rabbits and chickens," wrote Angie, who followed a dream and love, and left the city to live in the country.

EXPLORATION: Authentic Woman, Authentic Voice

This is a two-part exercise. First, using just a few words or a phrase, make a list of all the times you felt your most authentic, honest Self, all the times you felt most powerful or most complete. Allow these experiences to come intuitively; chronology doesn't matter. You may remember one time from when you were a kid and then a time from three weeks ago. Just write them down, as randomly as they appear. Remember: no thinking. Thinking blocks intuition.

After you've completed your list, close your eyes and let it settle. Take a few deep breaths as if erasing from memory the list you've just made.

For part two of the Exploration, open your eyes, scan your list, and select one of the items for an extended writing practice. If you want the intensity of a timed writing, set your alarm for fifteen or seventeen minutes. Otherwise, just go as long as the writing is pouring out. But remember, don't stop to read what you've written until you've finished.

Do this Exploration as often as you want, each time selecting another item from your list and exploring deeper those times when you feel most authentic. Notice what each experience has in common with the others. This is important information, a map to what matters most to you.

Approaching this Exploration another way, try writing about a time when you felt most alienated from your true nature.

Hearing Our Wild Voice

When we lose touch with our wild nature, we lose our wild voice. When we become too domesticated, when we become too involved with the outside world, when we try to live a "normal" life, to live up to what is expected of us by others and by ourselves, when we don't give ourselves time or solitude or deeply satisfying pleasures, whatever they may be, we sacrifice our authentic voice.

Sometimes that natural, wild voice gets trained out of us. I've worked with many a tech writer, as well as editors and writers, who earn a living cranking out PR pieces or marketing materials or clever advertising copy and who have a difficult time letting go of their "professional" voice. I've also known school teachers who spend weekend hours grading their students' written essays until their own writing can't pass their red-pencil test. Others find their wild voice tamed by the requirements of their profession: lawyers and paralegals, science writers, computer programmers, journalists.

It's not unusual to come across a writer who is afraid of her own wild nature and consequently finds her writing squeezed into the tiniest, most passive verb. "Good girls don't..." the voice in her head begins. "Better not..." it says, warning of risks unseen. "What would (fill in the blank) think?" Or perhaps some schoolteacher — the one who spends her weekends grading papers — slaughtered our authentic voice, the evidence of the carnage in ink red as blood right there on the page. Or somehow, because of family, religion, partners, or comments from a writing group, we've become so shy about the wildness of our deep voice that we hide our poems or sneak a few penciled words in a secret journal. Or, having written something we judge as dangerous, we tear the page out of our notebook and burn it. Maybe we incinerate whole notebooks, afraid that our true nature might be discovered. I once said I didn't want my mother to read the novel I was writing, not only because of what I'd written but because I didn't want her to know I was capable of having such thoughts.

And yet, like flowers pushing their way through the smallest cracks in concrete walls, our wild voices find their way to the light. In feudal Jiangyong County in the Hunan province of China, uneducated peasant women developed a separate written language, called Nüshu, meaning "female writing," which for a time was thought to be an espionage code. Perhaps in some ways it was, though rather than spying, these brave women were communicating among themselves.

I once knew twins who'd created their own secret language; perhaps they divined it in the womb. My best friend Betty and I, pulsing with adolescent wildness, developed a code so that we could send our renegade messages to each other. My sisters and I spoke pig Latin at the dinner table, believing our parents couldn't understand.

This wild voice, this expression of our deepest and most authentic selves, remains just beneath the surface of our most covered-over, tamed-down, pent-up, tongue-tied language. But

NOTES FOR NURTURING WILD VOICE

Wild voice is natural to us all, but even the most experienced writer will tell you it doesn't always come naturally. Like a garden, sometimes it requires our attention, and sometimes we have to get out of its way and let it do its own wild and natural thing.

Following are a few reminders of how to develop and nurture your wild voice. Each chapter will feature additional suggestions, ideas, and tips. I hope you'll try them all.

- Write often; practice daily.
- Freewrite.
- Take risks. Don't stop when your hand gets shaky.
- Remember to breathe.

so what if our voice is scratchy, or if it just naturally wants to sing those minor notes or needs to wail the blues? So what if it speaks in rhymes or fables or erotica or animal sounds? Our work as Wild Women is to bring it to light, give it breathing room, and listen to what it has to tell us. Who knows what we might discover?

"Sometimes," Gina said, "when I've hit just the right stride on a piece of writing and the words are flowing through me, I get a glimpse of my connection with the Universe."

Naming Ourselves

We are often asked to identify ourselves by our name, not only on public records — birth certificate, driver license, voter registration, income taxes — but also as a way of introducing ourselves to others. We sign our letters with our name. We put our name in sugary letters on birthday cakes, inside our clothes when we go to camp, and on our suitcases when we travel the world. A few of our oldest surnames were taken from the work we did or the craft we performed: Miller, Carpenter, Shoemaker. And some names came from the geography of where we lived: Brooks, Woods, Townsend.

Among some cultures a person's name may change when certain character-evolving events take place. Members can take on a new name when they feel ready for one or when a talent or new interest arises. A name doesn't have to be Judy or Erica or Gabriella. It can be whatever truly expresses who and where you are right now. "A name should be taken as an act of liberation, of celebration, of intention," said Erica Jong in *Fear of Fifty*. "A name should be a magical invocation to the muse. A name should be a self-blessing."

I COME FROM

Trudy Campbell
Wild Women Writing Workshop (2006)

I come from a place I do not know. My life thus far has been spent searching for the concrete, and yet intangible, heart of who I am. I am so much more than where I was born, to whom, at what time and place; and my evolution into Wild Womanhood deserves a ceremony, a proclamation to the Universe.

EXPLORATION: My Name as Blessing

As our next act of Claiming Wild Woman, let us name ourselves. I discovered the following writing exercise in Susan Wooldridge's delightful book *Poemcrazy: Freeing Your Life with Words.*

In our workshops, we take about two minutes on each prompt. Setting a timer can help focus the writing and often creates an intensity that can be the source of some surprising responses.

> *My real name is...*
> *Yesterday my name was...*
> *Tomorrow my name will be...*
> *Secretly I know my name is...*
> *I come from...*
> *This is the sound of my voice...*

If you really want to hear the sound of your voice, try reading what you've written out loud. I recommend doing this for all our writing. More than just the actual sound of your voice, the feel of the words in your mouth, the taste of them on your tongue, will tell you when you're writing in your authentic voice. You'll feel strength in the language, the rhythm will be yours, maybe the same as your breath or your heartbeat; it will be your natural rhythm, and your spoken voice will resonate with a truth that comes from inside you.

Also, when we read our work aloud, whether or not anyone is listening, the emotional content of what we've written will strike a deeper chord; we may or may not respond emotionally while we're writing, but give those words voice, and the emotion carried within them will emerge. When we are in tune with our wild nature, we write from that voice, with trueness and ease, a natural voice. When we are not connected or in tune, our writing can be stiff, unnatural, stilted. We won't believe it ourselves, and neither will anyone else who might read what we've written.

Claiming Wild Woman

When we name ourselves Wild Women and affirm our affiliation with our wildish nature, we may take up what we left behind long ago. We may return to making art, to dancing, to singing, to climbing trees. We may clear out a space that has cramped our style, creating a Wild Woman lair where we write and write and write — that novel we've wanted to begin, our memoir, a book about cooking vegan. We may become poets, playwrights, puppeteers. We may leave that job that doesn't suit us and find new work that fits as if it were custom-made — and maybe it will be.

We recognize the now-familiar voice of our inner wild nature and respond to it. We explore our deepest desires. We say yes! to ourselves and no to whatever or whomever distracts us from our true calling. And we go with joy, with anticipation, with excitement. If we are timid, if we are afraid, we ask ourselves, as Barbara did, "Why am I so afraid of her, my wild self, when I know she waits so kindly and patiently for me and she's the one who can connect me with my heart? She *is* my heart."

Continuing the Journey:
Further Explorations into Claiming Wild Woman

1. You placed a token or memento representing your wildish nature on your altar. Though you may not know why you chose this particular item, something about it called to you. In your Journey Notes, write about the piece. You may want to start with a description of it, of its shape or colors or smell, or where and how it came to you. Every object has a story. Write the story of your Wild Woman token or memento. Give it voice, if that feels right, letting the piece tell its own story.

2. Victoria wrote, "The moon would wake me up. I'd throw a blanket around my shoulders and go see. All that white light throwing strips across the walls and chairs and couches — drove me crazy. Made me restless. I wanted something I couldn't name."

   Close your eyes and remember what gives you a taste of your wildish nature; write what brings about longing in you.

3. Write about what you miss when you forget your wild self, when you forget to tend the creative cook fires, when life calls you to be "in the world" for too long and you don't have enough alone time or dreamtime.

4. From *Women Who Run with the Wolves*: "For some women air, night, sunlight, and trees are necessities. For others,

words, paper, and books are the only things that satiate.
For others, color, form, shadow, and clay are the absolutes.
Some women must leap, bow, and run, for their souls crave
dance. Yet others crave only a tree-leaning peace." What is
the basic nutrition for your soul? Write it. Experience it.

5. How do you adorn yourself? Do you have an outfit or a
piece of clothing in which you feel most yourself? Some
know me by my earrings, others by my cowboy boots. Do
you dress for fashion and the current style, or do you make
your own authentic statement?

Begin with the prompt: I dress myself in...

6. Write the story of your name. Where did it come from,
what does it mean, how does it fit you? Or how doesn't it?

Notes from the Journey

1. Did you write your Journey Notes every day? If not, did
you make a conscious decision not to write, or did time just
"slip by?"

2. Did you create and furnish your Wild Woman space? What
did you use to make it yours? Do you change or add to it
daily, or did you leave it in its original state?

3. Do you claim your authentic wildness every day in some
way — by being in touch with your body, by nourishing
yourself, both body and soul, by going outside and letting
nature touch you? Wild needs wild. Do you connect with
your pack? Do you acknowledge an accomplishment or
connection? Do you play, laugh, weep if you need to? Do
you dream? Howl? For those of us who don't tend to our
wildish nature as a natural part of our day, it may take some
conscious effort to begin nurturing ourselves in this way. I
hope you will make the effort.

3 WILD CHILD, WILD GIRL
Initiation and Forgetting

Venus is kind to creatures young as we;
We know not what we do, and while we're young
We have the right to live and love like gods.

— Ovid

Memory, soft edged and pastel. I am standing next to my mother, who is busy at the kitchen sink. I'm excited about something, and I must tell her about it. These few details: her apron, her hair in pin curls, the smell of dinner cooking, but no more. What is she doing? Washing dishes? Peeling potatoes? What had I seen or heard or experienced that I so urgently wanted to share? I can't remember. Then parts of the memory become more distinct — her hand on the top of my head (I didn't come much above her waist then). Her hand, not harsh, but solid, resting there. "Settle down," she says. "Just settle down."

Though I don't recall most of the details of this incident, the feel of her hand on my head, holding me down, her words — "settle down" — these details are alive even now, more than half a century later.

Here is Wild Child: responsive to the world, responsive to all her senses. Everything is an adventure, a discovery. She is creative. She is curious. She is physical. She is full of wonder. Sometimes she is too much.

In this chapter, we'll explore childhood and adolescence — our beautiful, creative Wild Child, alive with imagination, everything fresh to be discovered and learned, and our Wild Girl, strong, powerful, and creative. Making memory into story, we'll journey through our early years, what shaped us, who influenced us, and then, through initiation and individuation, how we began to shape ourselves.

What token have you brought to remind you of or to reflect Wild Child, Wild Girl? Over the many sessions of our Wild Women writing workshops, our Wild Child, Wild Girl altar has held tattered ballet slippers; charm bracelets; diaries, the kind with the lock and key; a tiny tea set; a worn baseball glove; a box of crayons; and so much more. In every item reside countless stories. If you haven't placed your memento near you, please take the time now to find something that will serve as your bridge from here to there — a relic that holds the essence of your childhood.

Wild Child

Our wildish nature shows up early in life. As children we often display a strong, instinctive pull toward something. Some of us are nature girls and love nothing more than being in the wild itself: paths and ponds and untamed places to explore, strange and fascinating creatures to study. We wear weeds in our hair and carry toads in our pockets. Others of us take to secret places with books to read, exploring the world through pictures and words, often making up our own stories. Art and music makers express themselves early in life — the girl with paint stains on her dress and scraps of colored paper stuck to her socks, the one whose feet can't be still beneath the dinner table or on the stairs, the singer whose voice precedes and follows her every move, the musician who beats out a rhythm on mama's pots and pans and Tupperware and who wants nothing more for her birthday than a brightly colored xylophone. We are a curious and creative bunch; we can't help ourselves. Creativity is natural to all human beings and especially so to those who cleave to their wildish nature. And if we're fortunate, we're encouraged.

At our young age, we dream we can be anything, and for us, wild girls that we are, it isn't a dream. We *know* we can be, because look at us: we are all a talented, creative, responsive Wild Child.

Listen to these Wild Women's memory fragments:

"Most of my fun came from playing make-believe with neighbor friends — acting out scenes we'd make up and perform with one another."

"I felt a strong calling as a girl to be a rodeo rider and roper."

"Ever since I was a child, I wanted to be a writer. I made up all sorts of dramas for my dolls and toy animals, and I wrote down stories as soon as I learned to write."

"I had a strong calling to be a baseball player. I hit a mean line drive, had a terrific swing, and was not a bad pitcher."

For me, beginning with reading *Brenda Starr, Girl Reporter* in the Sunday comics, I knew I wanted to travel the world on exotic adventures and write about them.

TWELVE

Mary Anita Winklea
Wild Women Writing Workshop (2012)

I remember standing in the yard
The grass still wet —
And the earth reeking
of the sweet, damp smell

from recent rain
Looking up in the sky my mind
still traveled trails
of words just read.
I longed to explore and claim new lands
Like sweet, strong Willa
and yearned to fly
like brave Amelia
Standing in the yard
on the great precipice
I did not know
I had wings

EXPLORATION: Write a Memory

Close your eyes and remember a time in your childhood when you felt a strong calling to do something, as if it were your destiny. You can write in a timed, focused freewrite if you want, setting your timer for seventeen minutes, or simply begin, letting the words free-fall from the memory itself and writing for as long as the memory wants to go.

Here's the prompt: I always knew I would...

Individuation: The Urge to Break Away

At a certain age, generally between ten and twelve, we are at a very powerful stage. We are old enough to have individuated some from our parents; we can go places away from home, such as camp or sleepovers. We're allowed certain freedoms and choices — how we want to dress, what activities to participate in. Many of us haven't begun to menstruate and we're not quite sexual beings, and though we may exhibit some of its signs and symptoms, we're not totally distracted by the physical and emotional aspects of puberty. We're girls, Wild Girls, precursors to what we can be as Wild Women.

Take a moment to remember who you were then. Close your eyes and allow an image of yourself at this time to arise. Maybe you're doing something clever and industrious: building a tree house or creating a science or art project. Maybe you see yourself dressed a certain way, in an outfit that makes you feel good and strong, and you remember its color exactly and the texture of the fabric. Maybe you're riding your bike or your horse, or you're at an overnight with your girlfriends, daring to stay up all night. This was the age when Carol, the woman who wrote about wanting to be a rodeo rider, remembered, "Galloping at full speed down a country road gave me my first sense of real freedom and personal power." For me, it was roller-skating, pushing off with strong legs, gliding over sidewalks buckled by tree roots, flying past small-town houses with yards tamed by picket fences. First the roller skates, then the bicycle.

> ### NOTES FOR NURTURING WILD VOICE
>
> - Write through your tears, your fears, your anger.
> - Break the rules.
> - Write words that feel dangerous, wild, exciting. Make lists of them; write them in large letters, bold colors.
> - Go to the edge of what feels comfortable. Leap!

Let an image come that shows you as this strong and powerful Wild Girl. In your Journey Notes, describe her. What is she doing? What is the look on her face? What are her thoughts or feelings? Take a few moments to be with her, to appreciate her strength, her passion.

For some girls, this is also the age, just as we're really beginning to fly, when our wings are clipped — that is, if they haven't already been clipped. Sometimes all it takes is a look, a gesture, a subtext we don't completely understand but that embeds itself in our psyche. "Are you sure you want to wear that?" "Do you think that's a good idea?" "Oh, I don't know…" the words trailing off with a worried shake of the head. Other times we're told out and out, "Oh, no you didn't."

This is when we begin to mistrust our natural instincts, and if it hasn't already begun, which often it has in some form or another, the domestication process is seriously under way. "Childhood is the first, inescapable political situation each of us has to negotiate," the poet June Jordan said.

GIRL

Jamaica Kincaid

Wash the white clothes on Monday and put them on the stone heap; wash the color clothes on Tuesday and put them on the clothesline to dry; don't walk barehead in the hot sun; cook pumpkin fritters in very hot sweet oil; soak your little cloths right after you take them off; when buying cotton to make yourself a nice blouse, be sure that it doesn't have gum on it, because that way it won't hold up well after a wash; soak salt fish overnight before you cook it; is it true that you sing benna in Sunday school?; always eat your food in such a way that it won't turn someone else's stomach; on Sundays try to walk like a lady and not like the slut you are so bent on becoming; don't sing benna in Sunday school; you mustn't speak to wharf-rat boys, not even to give directions; don't eat fruits on the street — flies will follow you; *but I don't sing benna on Sundays at all and never in Sunday school.*

This wonderful prose poem or story (it could be read as either) continues, with the girl being lectured on all the ways she must behave in order to become a woman and not just any woman, but the "perfect" woman. If you haven't read it, I hope you'll find it; it's widely anthologized. To me, it illustrates in a creative, delightful, and dramatic manner how wild girls are domesticated.

EXPLORATION: "You have to be carefully taught"

This is a two-part writing exercise. You can write each as a list or as prose. The writing may want to come out in dialogue or as the first wobbly construct of a poem. Let the work find its own form; trust the pen and the natural rhythm of the language. Dropping into the writing of this story may bring up some old anger or past hurt. Just keep the pen moving, letting the words come as they will.

Prompt for the first part: Things my mother never told me.

Write for fourteen minutes. Or freewrite as long as the energy is alive.

You may want to pause between part 1 and part 2, or simply let one flow to the other.

Prompt for the second part: Things I never told my mother.

Initiation: Girlhood to Womanhood

Though some cultures have a ceremony to mark a girl's first menstruation, many of us were brought up to keep this life-changing event private. But we're finally beginning to break through the secrecy (and even shame) that many of us and our mothers, and most certainly their mothers, endured. Oh, the names we used for our periods — Aunt Flo, Aunt Ruby, Aunt Martha (all these aunts coming to visit), the curse, back in the saddle again, flying our colors, and dozens more — once again using a secret code to communicate with one another. "Can I borrow a *lipstick?*" we'd ask our girlfriends when we'd left home without a supply of tampons.

But listen to this beautiful description of the "time of the moon" from Luis Urrea's novel *The Hummingbird's Daughter*; read it aloud. "All the medicine people knew when the time of the moon was coming. The girls' lights grew brighter. Their breaths carried scents like distant flowers. Blue, copper, fire colors flew above their heads, and some of them bent the world around them as they walked. It was like looking through a curved glass. Butterflies and hummingbirds, even bees, knew when a girl was coming into her holy days."

When I started my period on the last day of school in sixth grade, my mother said, "A little bitty thing like you?" It was a question that made me think I somehow could have controlled this thing happening to my body.

Madaline wasn't the only woman who was "vehement about not getting it." Paula told me she thought she could simply refuse to have it. "It just won't happen to me." She was so certain! But sooner or later, "it" does happen to us; sometimes we are relieved, sometimes annoyed, and sometimes downright joyful, like Marina, who loves having her period. She says she feels so "juicy."

June, a Wild Woman from a writing workshop, wrote, "I was initiated into womanhood by my embarrassed mother when I first got my period at age thirteen. All she said to me was, 'Now you are a woman.' She said she would have traditionally slapped me across my face, as she was by her mother when she began menstruating, but because she was a 'modern mother' she wouldn't do that to me."

These days more mothers, as well as other significant women in a girl's life — godmothers, grandmothers, aunts, older sisters — are creating a ritual or celebration to mark this passage from girlhood to womanhood. A search of the Internet will yield many examples. When my granddaughter told me she'd started menstruating, I left a small red-ribboned planter with a miniature rose on her front porch, along with a copy of "Marvelous Menstruating Moments" by Ntozake Shange.

EXPLORATION: An Initiation

If you didn't have an initiation when you started menstruating, let this writing exercise be a belated one. If you did have a rite or ritual, write about it. Start wherever you want, and write for as long as you want.

Write about your first period.

A Time of Forgetting

There comes a time in puberty and adolescence, as Wild Child becomes Wild Girl, when we come close either to claiming our wildish nature or to allowing ourselves to forget.

Often when girls begin menstruating and become sexual or at least sexually aware, they begin to follow the crowd. What's in fashion matters. Being popular matters. Boyfriends matter. Until very, very recently, and certainly not everywhere even now, it was an especially difficult and confusing time for young girls who were attracted to other young girls. We so want to belong that we may sacrifice our authenticity, our wildness, and move away from what we love so passionately. Belonging becomes the goal, above all else.

Nicole, who spent her Wild Child years drawing, and who wanted to grow up to be like Charles Schulz, with her beloved characters appearing everywhere, writes, "Instead, I hit puberty, and got tired of having no friends. Or only one. I wanted to be pretty and popular, stride down the hallway arm in arm with a gaggle of friends...I wanted to spend my time with kids who laughed and passed notes...kids who hung out after school, whose parents didn't know where they were every minute of every day. Girls who were cool. Girls who didn't sit home drawing. Alone."

It's also at this age when the real competition begins and we try to follow the rules for whatever art has been our mode of creative expression — writing, singing, painting, drawing, performing. Pleasing others, receiving recognition, and winning awards become more important than making our own noise, especially if our original creative expression has been faulted, denigrated, or disapproved of, something that, even if only by a glance or a downturned mouth, can silence our wild voices.

No wonder these adolescent years are so fraught.

Our diaries become our confidantes. Secrets and confessions and vows of hatred and revenge are written in these private pages. Pledges of undying love, poetry that will later embarrass us but that in the throes of adolescent passion may be the only means of expression.

Mortified is a live performance event staged in various cities, in which people get up on stage to read passages from their old diaries. The concept has many spinoffs, including *Mortified Nation*, a documentary based on the live performances. (You can find more information at getmortified.com.) As for me, I'd never read my angst-filled diaries out loud to anyone, let alone to a large audience! In fact, in a fit of embarrassment at the sophisticated age of twenty-five, I burned them all.

EXPLORATION: Dear Diary

Were you a diary keeper? Do you still have your diaries? If so, take them out and read a few pages. Then write in response to them. Write as the woman you are today to the girl who wrote in that diary.

If, like me, you no longer have those diaries, or you never kept a diary, write a "Dear Diary" entry in the voice of that Wild Girl. Let your memory fade back to a time when a diary might have been your best friend; talk to her.

Rites of Passage

Maybe because the United States is such a mash-up of cultures, we don't have many formal rites of passage ceremonies beyond weddings and funerals. But other countries do have them, especially coming-of-age rituals. Some rites performed on young girls coming into their sexuality are incredibly cruel and maiming. Others are celebrated with feasting, songs, and dancing. In our country, during the Apache Sunrise Ceremony, a girl of fourteen dances for four days as her passage to adulthood, and Jewish girls participate in Bat Mitzvahs. In some

Latin American communities, girls of fifteen celebrate their *quinceañera*, and there is, still, in some circles the debutante ball. But some rites of passage aren't ceremonial; we just do them, creating our own transitions from one stage to the next.

In *Girls on the Verge: Debutante Dips, Drive-bys, and Other Initiations*, Vendela Vida wrote about getting a fake ID at fifteen and how, significantly, she had to step through a doorway behind a counter at an ice cream shop where the illegal cards were made. She named herself "Kaluha West," after her favorite drink.

RITES OF PASSAGE

Dorianne Laux

When we were sixteen, summer nights in the suburbs
    sizzled
like barbecue coals,
the hiss of lawn sprinklers,
telephone wires humming above our heads,
Sherry and me walked every block within five miles that
    year,
sneaking into backyards, peeking through windows,
we dared and double-dared each other from behind the
    redwood slats.
Frog-legged, we slid down street lamps,
our laughter leaving trails of barking dogs behind us.
One night we came home the back way,
perfectly sexy walks and feeling "cool,"
and found my little sister on the side porch,
hiding between the plastic trash bins in her nightgown,
smoking Salems,
making Monroe faces in a hand-held mirror.

EXPLORATION: Rites of Passage

When we don't have a formal rite of passage, we must create our own, even if we don't realize that's what we're doing. Looking back we might see a history of sneaking out bedroom windows, building bonfires and jumping over them, changing our names, even if just within our circle of friends or in our diary. Getting our driver's license is a rite of passage, and so may be our first drink, first dance, first date, first time.

Roll the film back over those Wild Girl years and watch yourself performing some rite of passage. Write its story. Remember as you're writing to reach out and grab a passing detail — a smell or sound (weren't we always accompanied by a soundtrack during these years?); remember the feel of the air, colors, textures, expressions. Let your verbs dance with the music, capture dialogue. Bring the story alive with your wild voice.

Continuing the Journey:
Further Explorations into Wild Child, Wild Girl

1. In *Women Who Run with the Wolves*, Dr. Estés wrote about "stories that needed to be told outside the hearing of grown-ups." Write your own stories that, maybe even today, need to be told outside the hearing of the ghosts of those grown-ups.

2. Grown-ups also have stories they tell when they believe they are outside the hearing of children. "Little pitchers" and all that.

   Here's an excerpt of a piece I wrote about crawling beneath the table while my mother and her friends were gathered for their morning coffee klatch.

When you were small you curled beneath the table, surrounded by knees, your head tucked, invisible, and listened to their talk of war and men and how to cook a roast and roast a chicken and maybe lemon cake for dessert. And men again.

Husbands who snored who wouldn't talk who smelled of gasoline and night jobs and earning a living, and sometimes other women.

Voices whisper and tongues click, somebody says, More coffee?

And someone else says, Just hold your nose.

And the women laugh and the scratch of match against cover and the long exhale of smoke.

Do you remember things you heard that you weren't supposed to? Times you sat on the stairs and eavesdropped or stood on the other side of a door the adults thought was closed?

3. In her book *Journal to the Self*, Kathleen Adams describes a "List of 100" exercise. Here are her tips on how to do it: "It's OK to repeat. Write as *fast* as you can. You *don't* have to write in complete sentences. It's OK to repeat (See above). Your entries do *not* have to make sense Just *get it down*!"

In this Exploration, make a list of one hundred "firsts," limiting your list to the time before adulthood.

After you rest your fingers from that flurry of writing, choose one first from your list and do an extended writing. If you have time, select another first and do another extended writing, for fifteen or seventeen minutes. Remember what Flannery O'Connor said — that if you survive childhood you have enough material to last a lifetime. In this list of firsts, you have a bounty. Keep the list in your Journey Notes notebook, and pull it out from time to time for another writing session.

4. During these years of adolescence, great friendships are formed. A sense of knowing — our intuition — draws us to our own kind, and with these girlfriends, we set out to explore the wider world, taste forbidden fruit, and dare the fire. For this Exploration, write stories about girlfriends. Describe them and describe yourself as you were with them.

5. Coming-of-age stories are a popular subject for books, films, plays, and memoirs. This is the time of lost innocence. What we once thought to be true turns out not to be. We have tasted of the tree of knowledge. Coming-of-age stories aren't restricted to our youth, but this is the time when most of us experience the first of many losses of our innocence. Write your coming-of-age story.

Notes from the Journey

1. Did you write your Journey Notes every day? Does the writing come more easily now? Do you notice any changes in your writing, in how you approach it, or in how you feel when you've finished? Generally, the more we practice, the easier the natural voice comes.

2. How many of the claims did you make on your authentic wildness each day? Did you pay attention to your body and notice sensory details? Did you get yourself outside? Did you take time for creative expression? Did you laugh? Have you added any items to the list that express how you claim your authenticity each day? If not, what would you add?

3. Does what you wrote about in the "I always knew I would…" Exploration have any echoes in your life today?

4 BODY WRITING
The Voice of the Senses

You do not have to be good.
You do not have to walk on your knees
for a hundred miles through the desert, repenting.
You only have to let the soft animal of your body
love what it loves.

— Mary Oliver

The body speaks its own language. In her essay "Department of the Interior," Native American writer and storyteller Linda Hogan calls it a "landscape of truth-telling." It's a living, changing thing that is part of us, but not all of us. The body holds us to the earth and abides in the physical world of the senses — it tastes, hears, smells, sees, and feels. Its rhythm is breath and heartbeat. And somewhere within this skin-wrapped container of blood and bones and muscle dwells our history and the memory of our ancestral past. The body is storyteller. In Body Writing, we will give it voice.

Did you notice the dance of the flame when you settled into your writing space and lit your candle? Did you get a whiff of sulfur from the match you used to light it? What did you bring with you to your space as you began your work? A cup of coffee or tea? Did you savor its taste, its aroma? Do you have music playing in the background?

I ask these questions because as we move into Body Writing, we need, more than ever, to be attuned to our senses. Our awareness comes through our senses, and it is in the senses that our emotions reside; we don't just see, hear, touch, smell, taste; we respond to this sensory information with feelings — the anticipation of pleasure at that first sip of tea, the audible sigh as the soft notes of the guitar soothe away tension we didn't know we carried.

"Most people think of the mind as being located in the head," Diane Ackerman wrote, "but the latest findings in physiology suggest that the mind doesn't really dwell in the brain but travels the whole body on caravans of hormone and enzyme, busily making sense of the compound wonders we catalogue as touch, taste, smell, hearing, vision."

As you begin this chapter of writing from and about the body, spend a few moments settling into your body. Take a sensory inventory of your surroundings, breathing deeply and releasing any tension you may be holding. Close your eyes and spend a few moments in meditation, aware of your breath as it flows in and out and noticing places in your body — the way the soles of your feet touch the floor; the support of the chair against your sit-bones, hips, and back; the strength of your spine; how your neck holds the weight of your head. Notice other parts of your body — your shoulders, arms, hands. Take as long as you like; create your own body meditation. Can you feel your body's completeness? Can you feel the connection of your body to the body of the earth?

On my altar are six gemstones given to me by my friend Anita to bring on writing retreats. I pick up the stones one by one and rub my fingers over their polished bodies — the pure-white selenite, the smooth blue lace agate, the egg-shaped

Shiva Lingham, my favorite carnelian — I love to say its name. I hold the labradorite to the window and peer into its translucence to find the flashes of blue amid the green. I like the heft of the cube-shaped brown-and-white aragonite that is said to aid in pulling differing elements together in order to explore new possibilities. Each stone holds qualities a Wild Woman writer might need as she does her work. Rubbing each stone and meditating on its qualities brings me into the present. Me in my body, ready to begin the work.

Memories Held by the Senses

Body memories: the first crackling fire of fall when images of that time at the cabin in the mountains arise like the catch of flame. The old, familiar scent of Chantilly dusting powder, and there is Grandmother in her Sunday dress with its jet-black buttons. *That* song on the radio, and in comes the memory of love's first dance and its bittersweet farewell. The taste of spring's first strawberries; the twinge of pain at an old basketball injury; the scratchy feel of his old sweater you wear over your pajamas; the smell of him still held by the wool — every sensory image brings an already lived image. As I write this, a bee buzzes frantically against the windowpane, and I feel the sharp needle of pain on my side where I was stung by the bee that blew in through the open window of my car more than twenty-five years ago.

Our senses take in, our memory responds, sometimes with an image that appears lightning fast and disappears so quickly we're not even conscious of it. At other times we're transported to another time and place, with details so real it's as if we're living that time again. Or maybe, as imagination takes cues from memory and adds its own creative touches, we live it for the first time. This is the place where story resides and where our writing can find a toehold.

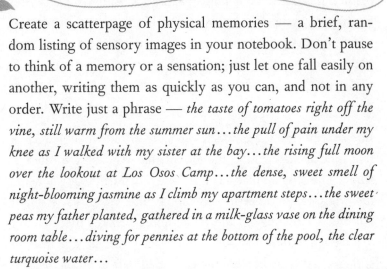

EXPLORATION: Sense and Memory

Create a scatterpage of physical memories — a brief, random listing of sensory images in your notebook. Don't pause to think of a memory or a sensation; just let one fall easily on another, writing them as quickly as you can, and not in any order. Write just a phrase — *the taste of tomatoes right off the vine, still warm from the summer sun...the pull of pain under my knee as I walked with my sister at the bay...the rising full moon over the lookout at Los Osos Camp...the dense, sweet smell of night-blooming jasmine as I climb my apartment steps...the sweet peas my father planted, gathered in a milk-glass vase on the dining room table...diving for pennies at the bottom of the pool, the clear turquoise water...*

Write these phrases as they come to you any place on your page. They don't have to be orderly, line by line. In fact, the memories may come more readily if you fling them anywhere on the page rather than trying to order them.

After you've spent several moments creating a montage of sense memories, close your eyes and be still, taking a few deep, slow breaths, letting the intensity of the exercise and the wellspring of memories settle. Then, when you're ready, open your eyes, choose one of the sense memories (notice which one pulls you, which you push away. The one you push away may be the one you are to write about), and open to a clean page in your notebook and begin writing. You can begin with the phrase itself or with another detail that comes from the memory.

Write for seventeen minutes, setting the timer. Or if you prefer, freewrite for as long as the writing has energy. Keep your scatterpage close at hand, and use the sense memories any time you want a writing prompt. Remember to get out of your own way as the words find their way onto the page.

Close your eyes and let your finger find another sense memory on your scatterpage. Give it another go, just for a few minutes, while you're still present with the language of your senses.

Vivid writing and wild voice come through the senses. Nobody else experiences the world exactly as you do. For all the sameness of our bodies, no one has the exact mash-up of DNA as you. You are the only one who creates that particular memory when you experience that sensation. Yes, my sisters and I all remember the sweet peas that grew on vines in Daddy's yard, but none of the others will describe the smell or colors exactly as I will; none of them will have the same memory of the sweet peas in the milk-glass vase, of Daddy's hands as he picked them, of Mother's as she arranged them in the vase and placed them on the maple table. This is where my wild voice takes over and tells the story as I remember it. And the closer I hew to specific sensory details, the more life the writing will have.

Look closely at the varied coloring on the petals of certain flowers that seem to lead to or come from the center of the blossoms. These markings act as a sort of superhighway for roaming bees, leading them to the nectar deep inside. The same can happen for you. Your senses will never let you down when you're circling around your writing looking for a detail that will lead you inside to where the juice is found.

Our Bodies, Our Selves

A journal exercise I've practiced for many years suggests a dialogue with the body. In the exercise, the journaler asks her body what it would like to say to her and waits, pen at the ready, for an intuitive response.

The first time I did this, I was knocked over by the vehemence of my body's response. It was so angry with me for the careless way I'd treated it, smoking and drinking too much, for my unhealthy diet, my candle aflame at both ends. The words that still pulse in one of those ancient journals stashed away in my storage unit told me in no uncertain terms that I'd taken my body for granted. Certainly, I had not treated it as the temple I'd been told it was. That dialogue was the beginning of many conversations I've had with my body.

Recently, I asked some Wild Women what their body would say to them if it could speak. The responses went from "Oh, she'd have a thing or two to say" to "Take care of me" to "Would you please just accept me, already!" Nicole said her body would write her a letter on apple-green stationery, and Josie's body said, "Wow! You sure have been through a lot, girl." Kim, a dancer, believes her body would say, "Thank you for listening." As for Karin, she reports that she and her body aren't on speaking terms these days.

EXPLORATION: Voice of the Body

For this Exploration, on a clean sheet of paper in your Journey Notes, ask your body if she would like to dialogue with you. When she responds, let her speak in her own voice, and then you can ask another question, or make a comment, the two voices going back and forth as if you're writing dialogue for a play or script. You may feel self-conscious at first, but if you give yourself over to the Exploration, who knows what drama or comedy or tragedy you might write or what information you might receive. Here's an example of a quick dialogue I just completed in my notebook.

JR: Good morning, dear body. Would you be willing to have a dialogue with me?

BODY: You know I'm not very happy with you right now, don't you?

JR: I can imagine why.

BODY: Can you?

JR: Well, the way I've been treating you lately. Not eating balanced meals…

BODY: Balanced? I don't think you even know what that means.

JR: (lightly) Something other than popcorn for dinner?

BODY: Very funny.

JR: You like salads, all that fruit…

BODY: (interrupting again) I also like to move. Get up! I want to go outside. I want to take long strides under those trees in the park. I want to dance!

And so it goes until the dialogue ends naturally. (This one went on for several more exchanges, during which I made some promises I hope I can keep.)

Now it's your turn. Begin any way you like, but I find I often get an immediate response when I begin with the invitation in the form of a question: "Would you like to dialogue with me?"

How We See Ourselves

"I sing the body electric," wrote Walt Whitman in one of his most famous poems, and in "Song of Myself" he exclaimed, "I dote on myself, there is that lot of me and all so luscious."

Oh, Walt, how you do go on. As women these are not often the words we say about our bodies, much as we're encouraged to do so, in advice columns and on blogs, by life coaches. "If only," we say, some of us, most of us. If only — our hips, our thighs, our butts, our breasts, our noses, our hair, our lips — if only. We have so much to find fault with as ideals are paraded before us in movies and videos, on TV, all over the Internet, in magazines, and in ads on billboards that display twenty feet of gorgeous.

> **NOTES FOR NURTURING WILD VOICE**
>
> - Write what you remember.
> - Write what you don't remember.
> - Allow your handwriting to get out of control.
> - Write sensory details.

Donna, a participant in one of the Wild Woman writing workshops, said, "I'm happy to finally have arrived at a place where I can say, 'I love my body.' I say this now without all the disclaimers I applied when I was younger, all the 'ifs' I had to add previously. 'If only my legs were longer, my thighs thinner, my nose smaller, my hair curlier.' Today I look at photos of a younger me and wonder what all the complaining was about. I looked great."

Many years ago when I was in Toastmistress, one of our tasks was to give a "how-to" speech. I don't remember mine, but I do remember a woman who talked to us about drawing. It was all in the seeing, she told us. She asked us first to draw our hand, which we did and, of course, I wasn't surprised when my sketch looked nothing at all like a real hand; it was just an outline of a hand with the fingernails drawn in. The speech-maker then told us to put our real hand next to our paper and really look at it — and to draw what we saw. While not quite as amazed as I was at seeing my vagina in a mirror at a long-ago consciousness-raising group, I was pretty surprised at how lifelike my hand looked, how much it resembled *my* hand — creases and shadows where bones were, the ribbons of veins and the shape of tendons beneath the skin, the slight tan line from the recently discarded wedding ring. All because I really looked.

When describing people in stories, fictional or otherwise, I always tell students to look for that telling detail. What is it about this person, this character, that is specific to her? Does she have a loud laugh? Or does she laugh "in a foghorn-like blast that drew stares in public"? (Mary Karr). Is he tall and good-looking or does he have "the wholesome good looks of the nice one in a boy band"? (Rebecca Mead).

Or maybe "he moves delicately, seeming to hover rather than stand: he has about him the distant, omniscient, ectoplasmic air of the butler in a haunted house" (Larissa MacFarquhar).

Or perhaps she resembles this character: "She wore her usual Betty Grable hairdo and open-toed pumps, and her shoulders had an aura of shoulder pads even in a sleeveless dress" (Margaret Atwood).

EXPLORATION: Character Description

In this Exploration, you're the character. Step back from how you might describe yourself to a stranger who's to meet you at a café — *five-foot-five, blonde, wearing a green jacket* — and describe yourself as though you're describing a character in a story. Let all your self-knowledge and years of mirror gazing drop by the wayside, and look at yourself from a different perspective. Instead of stating common characteristics, write what is unique (well, everything, but what is *really* unique), the "telling" detail, the detail that provides subtext and backstory. Use the language of your wild voice. Write how you walk, how you lounge against the wall, the sound of your voice, the curve of your neck. Play with this in a one-page character description.

If you had fun with this exercise and discovered something about yourself you might not otherwise have noticed, try another one. Write a description of yourself as your best friend might describe you, or your mother, or your significant other. Imagine Margaret Atwood casting you in one of her stories, or Rebecca Mead writing about you in *The New Yorker*. Be a mythical character with snakes for hair or wings of gold.

The Body Loves What It Loves

Flying down the hill on a bicycle, striding along a wooded trail, dancing, playing tennis, practicing yoga, running at dawn alone or with a hundred others, swimming, floating, bobbing in the ocean, lying naked in the sun, making love. These are the pleasures of the body. *This* feels good, we say as we stretch out on our Pilates mat, or rock-climb a cliff, or hike to the highest peak and gaze at the jaw-dropping view below us. I love this, we sigh as we roll over on the grass and smell the mulchy earth under us or lower our bodies into the 104-degree water of a hot tub.

Massage me. Knead the sore right out of my muscles.

Slather on the lotion, the oils, the sweet-smelling salve. Touch me. Stroke me. Kiss me. Do more of that.

EXPLORATION: What the Body Loves

For this Exploration, close your eyes and breathe yourself into your body. Be present with it and listen as it speaks in its silent voice.

What does your body love? Let the images play across the screen of your closed eyelids. See the beautiful images of your body when it is right with itself. How does it feel when you "let the soft warm animal of your body love what it loves"? Write the feeling; describe the images of your wild body in the language of your wild voice.

Illnesses, Wounds, Injuries, Scars

If you want to find a story, write about a scar. Every mark on our bodies, every injury, wound, and disfigurement, every bit of damage contains a story. Writing these stories can pave a path to healing; writing about an injury or illness can relieve some of their attendant pain and stress. We can make peace with our wounded bodies through writing our stories.

"The act of writing creatively, of working on words so they say what you mean and so the words do their work upon you, is similar to the action of your immune system responding to heal a wound or disease, maintaining wholeness and encouraging optimum well-being," wrote poetry therapist John Fox.

Studies show that writing about stress, giving voice to our

pain, our illnesses and injuries, actually does aid in the healing process, which is why the practice is used in hospitals and treatment centers and in private healing practices.

THE PARTICULARITY OF MY BODY

Gina Cameron

Wild Women Writing Workshop (2008)

I conjure up the cells of my bone marrow construction crew,
descendent deep in my bones,
in the hollow places,
where my inner ends and deep is deepest.
Cell workers, clad in hardhats and overalls, steel-toed boots,
swing their metal lunch boxes.
Hi-ho, hi-ho, they sing,
filing into the field of marrow-land, healthy and happy
      to build
my blood brick mortar.

When I was a young girl, nearly every winter brought with it a bout of tonsillitis. My fever would soar frighteningly, and I experienced "fever dreams," dreams even more surreal than my childhood nightdreams, which have in themselves conjured some wild-voiced writing over the years. Several of my stories and poems have come from injuries and bruises, and I've listened to what others have written of their accidents and illnesses, most much more serious than anything I've experienced. Our bodies are amazing in the true sense of that word, in their strength and resiliency and their ability to heal themselves. But by the same token, we are also so susceptible, so vulnerable, so very, very fragile.

EXPLORATION: In Sickness and in Health

We've survived childhood, and every one of us has nicks and cuts and scars to prove it. We've experienced bruises and knocks and who knows what-all injuries, inside and out. We've been attacked by poisons and invaded by viruses. We've been sick and cured and relapsed from whatever it was. (Considering all this, and the fact that we survive, I can't help but think of Maya Angelou's poem "And Still I Rise.")

This Exploration asks you to write about an illness or an injury or a wound, even a headache, if that's what wants to be written. Make a list if you want, take an inventory of your illnesses, create a map of your scars. Give voice to this aspect of your body.

The Female Body: in Celebration

Margaret Atwood, a Wild Woman by anyone's lights and a brilliant writer, was invited by the *Michigan Quarterly Review* to contribute an essay to an issue that would be "entirely devoted to the subject of 'The Female Body.' Knowing how well you have written on this topic...this capacious topic," the letter went on. Atwood responded with a sly and hilarious satirical essay called "The Female Body," in which she addresses the "topic" in her finest feminist voice.

The female body has been and remains a "capacious" topic — written about, sung about, painted, drawn, statued, photographed, illustrated, tattooed, comic-booked, paper-dolled, baby-dolled, Barbie-dolled, celebrated, denigrated, and impersonated by any number of male bodies.

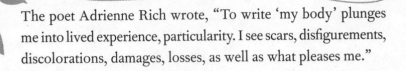

EXPLORATION: What Pleases You

The poet Adrienne Rich wrote, "To write 'my body' plunges me into lived experience, particularity. I see scars, disfigurements, discolorations, damages, losses, as well as what pleases me."

ODE TO MY HANDS

Mary Sue Doyle

Wild Women Writing Workshop (2006)

Bumpy, middle finger's plight.
Hold the pen, I have to write.
Smoothed-out fingerprints on left
Calloused from a guitar's stringed neck
Wire tendons, forearms fight
To pull the lines when tacking tight.
I watch these hands, my fingers splayed
In downward dog, "starfish" arrayed.

I am two hundred and six bones
And half in hands and feet.
My hands they pen this ode, this poem,
Scribble, pluck, tack, jump-back, repeat.

For this Exploration write about your body, its particularity, and remember especially what pleases you.

Continuing the Journey:
Further Explorations into Body Writing

1. Who in your family do you resemble? Do you have your mother's eyes? Your father's forehead? Do you have family

names for certain physical traits? The "Armstrong ear" or the "Hempy hips?" Who do you wish you looked like?

2. Focus on a favorite activity. How do you experience it through sight, smell, sound, touch, and taste? Write a paragraph using each of the senses, or integrate all the senses into one piece.

Generally as you revise, review your paragraphs, especially the descriptive ones, to see which sense you use most frequently and which you hardly use at all. If you use more sight details (as most of us do), change some of the references to other sense images. This will make for richer writing.

3. In "Wild Child, Wild Girl," we made a list of firsts. Add to that list "first sexual experience," "first orgasm." In all our writing Explorations about the body, we haven't included sex. This may be the time.

4. How do you dress yourself? What feels good against your skin? What fits your body, either literally or metaphorically? Are you comfortable naked? What part of your body do you hide or try to disguise? What do you like to show? Do you sometimes show off?

5. Four writing books on my shelves — *Succulent Wild Woman* by SARK, *Writing Wild* by Tina Welling, *Fruit-flesh* by Gayle Brandeis, and *Your Mythic Journey* by Sam Keen and Anne Valley-Fox — all suggest drawing an outline of your body on a large sheet of paper. SARK suggests making a sexual map, "as though you were creating an 'owner's manual' for someone else to read." Tina Welling said to "color in nature images and symbols on the body" as a way to enhance the relationship between your body and the earth.

For our Exploration, when you've drawn the outline of

your body, give different parts their own voice. Let your shoulders speak. What do your breasts want to say? Does each knee have a different accent? Your work might create a tone poem, or a series of monologues, a story in multiple parts.

One of the most powerful Body Writing experiences I've had is while participating (twice) in a Body Writing Retreat with friend and artist Pamela Underwood. In this retreat we make actual prints of our nude bodies using different media, then embellish the prints with words or esoterica or designs. You can find out more about Pamela's Body Writing Retreats at her website, pamelaunderwood.com.

Notes from the Journey

1. Do you look forward to the time you spend writing your Journey Notes? I hope so. Spending this time in quiet solitude, only you and your notebook, can provide a grounding to your day, whatever time you choose to do it.
2. Have you found your "pack?" We each need our own tribe, and Wild Women, however they express themselves, are yours. Have you noticed wildish aspects in some women you weren't previously aware of? Becoming more in tune with our own authentic nature, we are more able to recognize it in others.
3. Were any of the Explorations in the Body Writing work uncomfortable for you? Did you discover a voice that has been silenced or that speaks in a whisper? Sometimes the body speaks only in silences, but we must attune our senses to listen to these as well.

5 FAMILY
Fact and Fiction, Myth and Mystery

If you look deeply into the palm of your hand, you will see your parents and all generations of your ancestors. All of them are alive in this moment. Each is present in your body. You are the continuation of each of these people.

— Thich Nhat Hanh

As I begin to write, I feel my family around me, crowding, pushing and shoving, some of them; others are patient, some shy, some bold. That amalgam of genes, culture, and history, all those bodies — tall, squat, brown-eyed, blue-eyed, blind, probably, a few; children who would grow up to become old grandmothers, wrinkled and gray; and old grandfathers, stooped and smelling of grease and wood smoke. The aunts with their hair thinning or full, light or dark, up or down, curly or straight. The uncles, the ones who knew magic tricks and the ones who drank the aftershave; all the storytellers and story-makers, the hunters and the hunted, the dancers and the singers and the poets, the women who cooked and the ones who served and the ones who could wring the neck of a chicken. Here they all come. The candle is burning, it's story time. Who will be the first to tell?

"[Family] is the nest in which the soul is born, nurtured,

and released into life," Thomas Moore wrote. "It is an elaborate history and ancestry and a network of unpredictable personalities."

For Wild Women this nest is sometimes a welcoming place of nurturing and guidance, and sometimes it is a place filled with sticks and stones. But from whomever or wherever we come, our present is, in good part, made up of the stories of our past. These stories can be thought of as the twigs and string and odd detritus that holds our families together, and in each of these stories, at least one of these "unpredictable personalities" wants to take wing and fly.

One Flew East and One Flew West

I'm the kind of writer who believes that story comes out of character. That is, how a character responds to life, to situations, to events, is what makes the story, not a plotted-out trajectory that characters are manipulated into following. In my workshops I sometimes use the example of the character who needs to pay rent but has no money. The story will develop based on how the character goes about getting the money to pay the rent.

Would your character hie out the back door when the landlord comes knocking at the front? Would she or he call Mom to ask for the money? Rob a bank? Beg? Pray for a miracle?

So it is with the personalities who make up our family stories. Our family members' characteristics — physical, psychological, and sociological — propel them to believe and behave as they do: the black-sheep aunt who ran off with the circus, the older sister we admired for her ability to lie, the war-hero grandfather whose medals are elaborately framed and hung over the piano, the grandmother whose biscuits and jam feed our euphoric recall of childhood.

Families are entities, but they're made up of individuals, and one of the things about families is you get an opportunity, as writer Kendall Hailey put it, "to be intimately acquainted with people you might never even introduce yourself to, had life not done it for you."

EXPLORATION: One Flew over the Cuckoo's Nest

As we begin to explore and set to the page our family stories, let's bring to the present the people who make the stories "story": parents, grandparents, siblings, cousins, aunts, uncles, all those halfs and steps. Invite all of them to come forward, but rather than just writing their names and their labels, bring them to mind by writing short, declarative sentences about each one as you list them. Describe a habit, a characteristic, a penchant or prejudice. Describe a physical detail. Go for the singular and unique. Each of these declarative sentences suggests a story.

Begin with the name, and then write a simple sentence. For example, in my notebook, I wrote: "Great-grandmother Hempy had a mole on her chin as big as an eraser. Daddy closed his eyes and hummed when he danced with Mother. Sharon didn't let the foods on her plate touch. Janice left home seven times. Mother wore pin curls in the daytime and combed her hair out before Daddy came home. At six years old Amy could play her keyboard by ear. Aunt Ruth died of cancer. Uncle Harvey was the last one standing."

Keep going for as long as the names and unique details come to you. Leave space so you can continue to add twigs to your story nest. You may end up with a nest the size of an eagle's, but you'll always have another story to explore.

Probably, as you created your list, the stories began to beat their wings against your imagination, wanting to be told. Don't let them get away. Set aside time to write them. First this one, then the next and the next. Don't concern yourself with what it all might mean, or how the stories might come together. For now, just let them come forth, one by one.

Family Myths and Family Legends

Our lives are shaped by stories. Sometimes we create them on the spot — *Guess what happened today?* Sometimes we retell what has been told to us — *This is how our family came to California.* Using our imagination, we attempt to explain what we don't understand by adding details that later become part of the family history — *This is why Aunt Louise and Aunt Theresa can't be invited to the same party.* If a story is told often enough and for long enough and repeated down through generations, it can take on the elements of myth, revealing who we are, how we got here, and why we do what we do.

As storytellers, we naturally use metaphor, symbology, and imagination to make the story better. We writers are especially good at freestyling details. But it isn't just writers who embellish, embroider, and enhance; every storyteller does. My mother would never think of herself as a storyteller, but it is from her that I heard the tales of how poor the family was when she was a girl. Maybe, without being conscious of it, she wanted to relate certain values or mores about our history of hard-working, honest, salt-of-the-earth folks. On the other hand, she might have wanted to remind me of the kind of people we come from just in case I was getting fancy ideas or presenting myself in a way that didn't fit with her beliefs of who we were.

EXPLORATION: Down through the Family

Were you told the myth of your family origins, or have you, through the years, created your own myth by taking a little of this and a little of that and weaving it together to form something you can believe?

"We received our coloring from Norsemen," Astrid's mother tells her daughter in Janet Fitch's beautiful coming-of-age novel, *White Oleander.* "Hairy savages who hacked their gods to pieces and hung the flesh from trees. We are the ones who sacked Rome. Fear only feeble old age and death in bed. Don't forget who you are."

This excerpt is, of course, fiction and uses damned strong language to tell a young girl the story of her ancestors, but using mythic structure and phrasing is a way of going deeper, writing from an authentic place that sometimes must sacrifice fact in order to tell a truer truth.

In *Writing for Your Life*, Deena Metzger suggested beginning your story with a mythic phrase to "stimulate the mythic imagination: 'And it came to pass that...' or 'It is told that...'"

Try starting the myth of your family using one of these phrases, or another like it. Allow the story to come through you; find the metaphor within the myth that gives it depth. Does your family history contain legends that you've repeated? Sometimes even the most tenuous connection to a well-known person, hero, or antihero makes for the most oft-repeated stories, the antihero frequently being the most titillating.

One day my sister the genealogist asked if I had any stories or memories of our great-grandmother. I told her about a prose poem I'd written that tells a version of our family's Jesse James legend in which my great grandmother held a baby Jesse on her lap.

"It wasn't Jesse," my sister said. "It was Frank. Frank James is Jesse's brother, and she didn't hold him on her lap. He was older than her."

So maybe it was the other way around: Frank James held my great-grandmother on his lap. But that's not probable or even appealing as a family story. Nobody wants Frank James in their family legend. If they're going to have a good story, it needs to be Jesse. So my version of the James Family connection may be the one picked up and repeated by my children and grandchildren.

WHEN JESSE JAMES WAS A BABY

Once, a long time ago, my great-grandmother held Jesse James on her lap. This is what they told us, my father never breaking a grin.

I am banging ivory piano keys the same color as my great-grandmother's teeth, as the cameo brooch at her neck where black lace scratches mottled skin. She is anchored in her rocking chair by swollen feet, thick ankles, secure shoes. She breathes camphor.

Yes, she nodded. The wen on her chin like an eraser, pink and rounded, a thick black hair, straight as a pencil lead. Jesse was a baby then. Sweet boy, she said, and patted her ample lap where Jesse sat. Prettiest eyes.

We didn't know this about Jesse. We'd heard no mention of his eyes except that they stared unblinking from the bedroom floor, where he fell when he was shot dead.

But here is Grandmother in her chair beside the lace-curtained window that looks across the street to the Star Market with its metal sign squeaking in the wind.

Grandmother remembering the weight of Jesse's little bottom. What a shame, such pretty eyes.

Write one of your family legends. Let your imagination go freestyle, and add details that bring the story to life. Consider it voice lessons for your wild voice.

Family Secrets, Family Lies

We all have skeletons in our closets, some going back to a time before closets were part of a family's home. Some of this hidden or distorted past we may never know about, and some has become part of the tapestry that is our family history. There are the secrets we know, even if we don't talk about them, and there are others we suspect. We read facial expressions, voice intonations, body language. Even, or maybe especially, as children, our intuition tells us when something is amiss. Lying is not a foreign language.

Occasionally truth will be revealed through accident or circumstance.

Home alone one boring teenage afternoon, I found myself rummaging in my parents' closet, where admittedly I had no business being. Among old photographs, my dad's navy ribbons, and other mementos in a box on the floor of the closet, I discovered their marriage license, which revealed a different date from the anniversary I knew them to always celebrate. I still remember the heart-tripping moment of discovering that piece of paper and counting on my fingers from the date on it to the date of my oldest sister's birth. But because I had been schooled both subtly and explicitly in what was acceptable for discussion and what was kept secret, I played my part and never asked my parents about the discrepancy in the two dates.

Shame is a common reason for keeping secrets, which always results in telling lies. But shining a light, acknowledging the secret, unraveling the lie, if only for ourselves and to ourselves, takes us that much closer to our authenticity. For us writers, story is a way of shining that light, and when we write our stories, lies can become fiction that can tell a truer truth.

The following short short is from a fiction collection but illustrates how a writer might take a family secret and, using her wild imagination, turn it into a story.

MY MOTHER WAS AN UPRIGHT PIANO

Tania Hershman

My mother was an upright piano, spine erect, lid tightly closed, unplayable except by the maestro. My father was not the maestro. My father was the piano tuner; technically expert, he never made her sing. It was someone else's husband who turned her into a baby grand.

How did I know? She told me. During the last weeks, when she was bent, lid slightly open, ivories yellowed.

"Every Tuesday," she said. "Midday. A knock at the door." The first time, I froze. A grown woman myself, I listened to my mother talk and was back playing with dolls and wasps' nests. I cut my visit short. My mother didn't notice. She'd already fallen asleep.

The second time, I asked questions.

"Mother," I said. "He...came around. On Tuesdays. How many?"

"We are fallen stars, he said to me," whispered my mother, the formerly-upright piano. "You and me, he said. And then he would take my hand." She closed her eyes, smiled.

My father, the tuner, never took anyone's hand. He was sharp, efficient. I searched my mother's face for another hint or instruction. "Should I find myself one?" I wanted to ask. "A fallen star? A maestro? Am I like you?" But she had stopped talking and begun to snore gently. I sat with her, watching the rise and fall of her chest and the way her fingers fluttered in her lap, longing for arpeggios to dance across my stiffening keys.

EXPLORATION: Shining the Light

One of the exercises I offer in my workshops is an opportunity to write about a secret or lie. I pass out small slips of paper and have participants write a few details of a secret — a big secret, little secret, not-so-secret secret — on each strip. We fold the strips of paper and place them willy-nilly in front of us, mixing them up, mixing them up, mixing them up like a shell game so that we lose track of which secret is on which strip of paper. Then we select one from our pile to write about.

While I always invite writers to read their work aloud after each writing session, no one is ever required to read. This provides a certain safety and allows writers to explore the depths they might otherwise shy away from. And, for this particular exercise, I tell them they can tear up their pages after they've written the story if they want to. I even offer to burn the stories in the trash can. So far nobody has taken me up on this.

What I and others have discovered is that when we finally put the words on the page, the secret loses some of its power and becomes, instead, a story, which has power of a different kind.

IT RUNS IN MY FAMILY

Laurinda Enos

Wild Women Writing Workshop (2006)

I hardly knew my mother's mother. My family didn't talk about her very often, unless that's who they were talking about when my mother and my Aunt Pauline spoke Finnish. I had so few encounters with her that I don't even remember her nickname. Sometimes I called her "my Mummu," to distinguish her from my mother's grandmother, who everybody talked about....

Over time, I learned that my grandmother didn't get married and move out of her parents' house until she'd had four children. All girls. My mother was the second, all fathered, so it's told, by the same Irish man who my grandmother refused to marry. There were shock treatments with iced sheets to correct her wild behavior, settle her down. In 1935, when my mother was fifteen, my grandmother, then thirty-seven, married another man with whom she had two daughters and a son. My Aunt Pat, youngest of the seven, talks about the years when her mother stayed in bed all winter and ran wild in the summer.

They say depression runs in my family. I disagree. From everything I've heard it's a wild streak that runs in my family. A wild streak suppressed to the point of depression.

Try this Exploration yourself. Write from your intuitive voice, knowing you can tear the pages up after you've written. But also, because of your willingness to write from this riskier, authentic place, you may want to work with the story you've begun, revising, rewriting, and going deeper.

I took the piece I'd written from the discovery of my parents' secret and gave it to a fictional character; it became part of her backstory and when she remembered it, the secret gave her a new perspective about her parents, especially her mother and herself. It did the same for me.

Remember, creativity is all about wildness.

Our Parents, Our Selves

There comes a time in our lives as children when we discover our parents are individuals in their own right, that they have lives that don't include us. We overhear a conversation or observe a particular way they look at each other — the exchange of a glance or an intimate gesture that excludes us. This discovery is the seed of an ever-changing perspective of our parents that continues for as long as we are alive.

Though psychologists and theorists may organize the child-parent relationship by stages, complete with labels and predictions, our stories make them personal, and the details singular and particular. When we write from wild voice, it's those details we hold in our gaze and bring forth onto the page.

Mothers and Daughters and Mothers of Daughters

Every daughter has a mother. Some moms nurtured and encouraged our wildish nature, but some did not. If our mothers forgot their own wildness and gave themselves over to domestication, then messages both spoken and implied probably directed us down the same narrow path. Rather than being blessed with a confirmation of our creativity and natural responsiveness to the world, we were raised to "be obedient and quiet, to share and not be selfish, to always 'play nice,'" as Donna put it.

While risk taking is essential to living an authentic life, many of the women I asked said their mothers warned against taking chances or risking anything. In Suzana's family, "one was heavily encouraged to play it safe in every aspect of life."

But creative is not careful, and many of us, like Gina, strained against "the push-pull of my upbringing with my creative, rebellious temperament," which she said, "has been and continues to be a core struggle in my life."

"A daughter's relationship with her mother is something akin to bungee diving," wrote journalist Victoria Secunda. "She can stake her claim in the outside world in what looks like total autonomy...but there is an invisible emotional cord that snaps her back."

ANNIE JOHN

Jamaica Kincaid

Out of the corner of one eye, I could see my mother. Out of the corner of the other eye, I could see her shadow on the wall, cast there by the lamp-light. It was a big and solid shadow, and it looked so much like my mother that I became frightened. For I could not be sure whether for the rest of my life I would be able to tell when it was really my mother and when it was really her shadow standing between me and the rest of the world.

So it is here, in the territory of myth and legend, fairy tales and real life, lies and secrets, longing and fulfillment, heartache and heartbreak, and love of the rarest, yet most primal form, where we set upon our stories of mothers and daughters. Here we find material that arises from, as Adrienne Rich put it, "the deepest mutuality and the most painful estrangement."

If there has been a legacy of push-pull in our lifelong journey with our mothers — from infancy to adolescence to adulthood to perhaps becoming a mother ourselves — the stories we write will mark stress points and resting points along the span. But the same story, written at different times in our life, or hers, may take on new coloration and voice, and with this change in perspective, may turn out to be a completely different story. We see her differently because we ourselves have changed.

Sylvia wrote this about her mother:

> Brooklyn, New York, born and raised, she married at age thirty-five and was brought to a small town in Ohio and then a farm, by my Dad. I never thought of the courage it must have taken for her to make that leap and begin having children at age thirty-six and learning to cook for farmhands. I always thought of her as fearful — she had never been around animals, let alone livestock, she was used to the subway and the opera, lived with her mother until she married. But as I review her life, I see that she must have been more risk taking and pioneering than I thought, and on some level, that must have affected my own life. I wish I could tell her that now.

I have written and revised, ad nauseam, two novels and countless stories that explore my own mother-daughter history, and I don't expect I'm finished yet. Or ever will be. Whether she keeps changing (which is impossible; she's been dead for more than a decade) or I do, the stories continue to evolve.

Rich said, "It is hard to write about my own mother. Whatever I do write, is my story I am telling, my version of the past. If she were to tell her own story other landscapes would be revealed."

EXPLORATION: Daughters Writing Mothers

Do you have questions you haven't asked your mother, and might never have the opportunity to ask? Do you wonder what she was like as a child, what she dreamed of but never spoke about?

In a eulogy for my mother, I wrote,

> Did you really love fishing? Or did you just do it because Daddy loved it? What dreams did you give up to be his wife and our mother? I've always known you put away something of what you were to be, for what you thought you should be. I wish I could have known that other you. The one that perhaps came alive only in your early visions, long, long ago when you were young and anything was possible.

What do you know for certain about your mother, and what do you imagine? Take time for this Exploration, and in your reverie, allow images of your mother to come forth. Write them as they come, and explore their details for the undercurrents of a deeper story.

If you have photographs of your mother at different ages, examine them closely. Rather than the story you know about the photograph or the story you've been told, what story does the photograph tell?

EXPLORATION: Mothers Writing Daughters

I can't help but wonder, as I write about mothers and daughters and confess my complex relationship with my own mother, what she might have said or written about me. Not *to* me; I have plenty of memories in word-by-specific-word of her thoughts and opinions about me or my ideas or my behavior. I wonder what she might have said to my father about me, or to her mother or sisters or friends. She didn't keep a journal, and she didn't write, except for letters and brief notes on Christmas cards, but never a letter to me, even when I lived some distance away.

I write about my daughter frequently, ministories in my writing practice notebooks, braggy posts on Facebook, my concerns in my journal, where memories also find their way. If I resist the urge to toss all those journals, and if she happens to come across them clearing out the detritus of my past, and if she's not too awfully bored by the quotidian banality of most of the entries, she might find something of interest about herself.

In writing about her, I often discover or uncover something about myself, and more frequently than that reveal another layer in our mother-daughter relationship.

STONEHENGE AND THE LOUVRE WERE COOL
by Carol Lucci Wisner

A Saturday, in January: she sleeps till eleven, takes a lei-surely bath, tries on my earrings, uses my powder, my kohl pencils. Walks around in nothing but a man's shirt, blue plaid flannel, her friend Quinn's. Draws smudgy lines on her lids and studies the effect with her eyes half shut, her mouth loose, pouting. Does her laundry and lies on the couch, watching re-runs of "The Real World" — a documentary about seven incompatible people living in a beach house. Waits for her clothes to dry and for the phone to ring.

This is the child, I tell myself, who'd play happily in her playpen so I could go downstairs to throw another load into the washer, who wouldn't keep her shoes on in school, who was always losing her lunch money, who sucked her thumb when she thought no one was looking. Who is she now — this touchy stranger with whom I seem to have no history? She has kept a journal since she was six years old, and she writes poems that make the hairs on the back of my neck stand on end. At her feet, lying open on the floor, is a book, one I remember reading when she was just learning to run. I read it in five- and ten-minute installments.

Her aimlessness, her evident lack of a plan drives me crazy, and we're like two travelers stranded in a storm, stuck with each other. Her father's out of town and with him gone, I wonder — will there be no one to referee, or will the level of intensity ease up just a little? I don't know. I mean, it could go either way.

We get into a discussion about words people don't use much anymore. Crestfallen, abyss, bereft. Bereft. I say I think it's still a good word, but one I've never used, never spoken out loud. She says, "What are you waiting for?"

If you are the mother of a daughter, for this Exploration write about your daughter as she is now or how she was in a time

> **NOTES FOR NURTURING WILD VOICE**
>
> - Write from the body, be in the body, go to the body.
> - Get close to that raw place, close enough to hear its heartbeat, to smell it.
> - Write the wound, the scar, the sore spot.

gone by. Begin with the detail of a normal Saturday afternoon or school-day morning and expand on it. Write in the present tense, as Wisner did in her piece, even though you're writing of a past time. Using present tense brings an immediacy to the scene and can animate details.

Does your daughter look like you? Do you see a similarity in her gestures, the way she flips her hair back over her shoulder or stands with one foot on top of the other? Or is she (like you) a marvel of complications that leaves you shaking your head in dismay or weeping at your good fortune? Where do you recognize the Wild Child or Wild Girl in her? Is she a Wild Woman in her own right?

Fathers and Daughters: The Ideal and the Real

It's said that most three-year-old girls fall in love with their fathers; some even want their mother to disappear so they can marry their dad. Other girls grow into women who spend their whole lives searching for someone to watch over them.

Father is the archetype of the Elder, the King, the Wise One. He is Teacher, Magician, Defender of the Faith and the Realm. He is both Darth Vader and Dumbledore. He is Absent Father and Atticus Finch. Zeus and Milquetoast. He is all this and a thousand other faces — complex, contradictory, completely unique, and completely yours.

Throughout this book (and my life), I have written of my "father," and, in evoking childhood memories, "Daddy." Both titles describe his role in my life. He is the one who nurtured my curiosity and bragged on my accomplishments; he's also the one who slapped my face for lying. He, more than anyone else, encouraged my Wild Child yearnings and modeled braving the path that follows dreams.

Not all my sisters would say the same.

"It doesn't matter who my father was," Anne Sexton wrote in a journal, "it matters who I remember he was."

ALL MY PRETTY ONES
Anne Sexton

These are the snapshots of marriage, stopped in places.
Side by side at the rail toward Nassau now;
here, with the winner's cup at the speedboat races,
here, in tails at the Cotillion, you take a bow,
here, by our kennel of dogs with their pink eyes,
running like show-bred pigs in their chain-link pen;
here, at the horseshow where my sister wins a prize;
and here, standing like a duke among groups of men.
Now I fold you down, my drunkard, my navigator,
my first lost keeper, to love or look at later.

As I've written each of these sections exploring family I have placed a different memento or photograph on my altar, or invoked an image that would bring to mind aspects of relationship or particular memories of individuals: my young grandmother in her high, stiff-collared blouse with her hair done up, and another of her, older and thickening, standing beside the wildly blooming spirea in front of the family home; aunts and uncles and cousins gathered around the Christmas dinner table or at a family picnic; Mother pushing her hair off her forehead with her forearm, drenched in the summer sweat of canning.

Now, as we begin our written Explorations of Father, I bring to mind a photograph of Daddy posed on the Golden Gate Bridge in his navy uniform, its wide collar lifted in the wind.

EXPLORATION: Daughters Writing Father / Daughters Writing Daddy

No matter how many times or with how many groups I have used the prompt "My father's hands," the stories that result always surprise me in their freshness, their individuality, and their wild rawness. I've been using the prompt for so many years, I can't remember where I first heard it or the first time I wrote from it.

Try it for yourself as a simple writing-practice-style, timed, focused writing. Set your timer for seventeen minutes, write the prompt at the top of a blank page, and follow the first image that appears. Don't stop until the timer goes off.

After you've finished, breathe, read aloud what you've written, and follow up with whatever thoughts or feelings surface.

Continuing the Journey: Further Explorations into Family

1. I come from a family of four daughters, three of us in a three-year period; after a ten-year lull, the fourth arrived. Each of us played a different role in the family drama, and our relationships with one another still provide material for my work and blessings in my life. Again invoking Flannery O'Connor: "If you survived childhood..."

   If you have sisters, was there a time when you were wild children together? Or wild girls? What was your young relationship? How has it changed as you've become adults?

   If you don't have a sister, have you imagined what it would be like to have one?

   Nicole, an only child, wrote, "I savored slumber parties, sleepovers. I had no siblings so these were rare occasions to feel like 'one of the girls' and to imagine what it would be like to have sisters. Something about bunking together, sharing secrets in pajamas, seeing each other in our underwear, made me feel like part of something larger, an evolving community, an ad hoc sisterhood."

What about brothers? I don't have any brother-sister stories, but you may. Write them.

2. We haven't forgotten our grandmothers. These women who may have been like second mothers to us, or role models, or vestiges of Wild Women of an earlier time, like Jill's grandma, who "designed hats, watched Westerns, and played poker" and loved her unconditionally. They might have lived at a time when women weren't allowed to own property or to vote. Certainly they lived in a time different from ours.

Write the ways in which your grandmothers influenced you. What stories do you know of them and of their lives?

3. Do you ever feel like an outsider in your family, the one who doesn't belong? Were you ever called the "black sheep?" Or, like me, the "wild one?" Like me, do you ever secretly take pride in the name?

4. Sense memories are a door into stories. What was the smell of your grandmother's bedroom, your parents' car, the basement or garage of your family home? List the sounds you heard as a young girl in the morning when you awoke. What was the texture of the air in the kitchen in the summer, the carpet on the living room floor? What was for Sunday dinner? Let your sense memories lead the way.

5. Following are some quickie prompts for writing about families. Use these and make up some of your own, either

on slips of paper that you tuck into a container on your writing desk or in the back of your Journey Notes to pull up and write to during an impromptu practice session.

Write about comings and goings, who left and who stayed.

You're at a family meal.

My mother wore _____.

This is a story my father told me.

This is the language of my family.

Notes from the Journey

1. This is an especially long chapter, maybe even calling for a new Journey Notes notebook. Is all this detail about family and exploration into relationships stirring up stories that show up in surprising places while you are simply writing the day-to-day in your Journey Notes notebook? This is a good thing; who knows what might come of all these bits and pieces of memory and reflection?

2. If you made it all the way through this chapter on family, going on all the Explorations, and even taking some side paths off the main trail, now is the time to acknowledge what you've accomplished. And if you haven't quite finished all the writing, acknowledge the work you did do, and make a pact with yourself to keep the writing alive by coming back to it. If you skipped some of the Explorations, check in with yourself and ask why. Would rephrasing what you passed over make entry into the work easier or truer to your deep knowing?

3. Did you find it easy to access your wild voice in writing family stories? If not, keep writing, keep practicing; find

a trusted partner to write with or a group that can support you in the work. Writing from authentic wildness doesn't usually happen like the burning-bush phenomenon; it's more of a turn the soil, plant a garden, water it, be patient, and keep weeding kind of process.

6 WRITING PLACE
The Geography of Our Lives

We can't separate who we are from where we are. People are rooted in time and place, and so our psychic space is generously seasoned with memories of physical territories.

— Sam Keen and Anne Valley-Fox

The thing about us humans — wild or domesticated — is that we are physical beings in physical bodies, set down in physical places. Much as we might like to think of ourselves as spiritual beings — and maybe we are that, too — we are definitely, absolutely, without a doubt, physical beings. And, physical beings that we are, we are grounded in place. Even the eagle must find a place to land and build her nest.

Place is a fact of our lives. As Sam Keen and Anne Valley-Fox wrote, "we can't separate who we are from where we are."

Place influences how we speak, what we eat, and how we measure our days. It shapes our beliefs, our values, and our moral choices. Not only can we not separate who we are from where we are, but also, we are indelibly marked by where we have been. History and memory are rooted in place, and the map of our psyche is found in the geography of our past.

For our work in this section, we'll explore where we were born, places we have lived, and places that help define who we are.

If I had access to some, I would place a scoopful of rich dark Missouri dirt on my altar for this session. I would also place a cutting from a eucalyptus tree and a stem of bright magenta bracts from the bougainvillea that grows so gorgeously in my neighborhood. These tokens would ground me in my birthplace and in the place I choose to live now — one the place where I took root and the other the place where I matured.

My family moved to San Diego from northwest Missouri when I was a young girl, and I thought my dad had brought me home to paradise — the constant sun, the endless ocean, oranges that grew in our own backyard, and oh, those sexy Mexican American boys with their slim hips and dark eyes, with Mexico itself just across the border. But paradise or no, there was a time when I abdicated to Los Angeles and a time, somehow, surprisingly, when I wound up in Oklahoma, neither of which felt like home. I also settled in San Francisco briefly, lived in Barcelona for a couple of years, and located myself in Paris for a few frigid months during the winter of my forty-eighth year. I've been to countries in South America, Central America, and Europe. I've gone to Australia, Canada, and India, to Indonesia and Hong Kong. I've visited forty-eight of the fifty states, sometimes just passing through, sometimes staying awhile. I've entertained fantasies of living here or there, and there's a certain stretch between Baton Rouge and New Orleans that feels like a place I've lived in a former life. But I keep tapping the heels of my well-worn flip-flops and returning home to San Diego.

For Wild Women to be true to our authentic nature, like the eagle, like even the sparrow, we must find our place to land

and build our nest. This is true in a literal sense as well as a metaphoric. During the times I was in places that didn't feel like home, I often needed to retreat to a private, interior place to regain my equilibrium. Even in the place that is my chosen home, I need this solitary quiet time, which, most often, I find in my daily journal writing. It's here where I can relax against the natural rhythms of my heart and listen to the deep tellings of my intuitive voice.

Spirit in Landscape, the Soul of Place

In her beautiful essay "Walking," Linda Hogan writes about the mysterious language of nature — the sunflower that somehow knows the time to call the birds to come for its seeds, a certain kind of bamboo flower that, once every century, blooms, adding, "Whether they are in Malaysia or in a greenhouse in Minnesota, it makes no difference, nor does the age or size of the plant. They flower. Some current of an inner language passes between them, through space and separation, in ways we cannot explain in our language."

So certain places are with us. We can attempt to describe the landscape, what flowers there, what road passes through, how the sky looks when it rains, but the language we have for what connects us with place is more elusive than mere description, though that may be where we begin. But to attempt to understand and perhaps express the sense of inner-connectedness we experience, we must slow down and go to that deep place, and listen. To write a thing as mysterious and soulful as the sense of being at one with ourselves and the place we inhabit requires us to retreat into our interior where wild and wild converse.

In her essay Hogan quoted John Hay, who wrote, "There are occasions when you can hear the mysterious language of the Earth, in water, or coming through the trees, emanating from the mosses, seeping through the undercurrents of the soil, but you have to be willing to wait and receive."

DIDGERIDOO

Janet Baker

Hot Nights, Wild Women Writing Workshop (1997)

I have been droning
a piece of tree
it's talking back to me
eucalyptus language
tells me this is my life now
awakens me like the buzz
of my own snoring
only need to breathe and blow
at the same time,
run my body with
animal sounds
paint it platypus and lizard

EXPLORATION: Walking

Close your eyes and take an imaginary walk through a remembered landscape, breathing slowly and listening deeply, seeing with the deep vision that emanates from your wild nature. Let the words and images come as they will, without attempting to shape them. Let whatever or whomever has come before speak through you. Give language to the voice of the landscape. Watch and listen, and write.

Place as Memory

Memories are rooted in place: a lifetime of kitchens, backyards, porches, and patios. Our bedroom and our best friend's bedroom, the street where we played until dark and our parents called us inside, the park where we picnicked, the swimming pool with its aquamarine water smelling of chlorine or the pond on the farm with its muddy banks. If you want to enter a memory, enter a room in your grandmother's house. Remember an incident, and the place where it happened will figure prominently in the story. Everything happens somewhere, and if you want to bring the memory alive, be in the place where it occurred.

In her essay "Place in Fiction," Eudora Welty writes, "Location is the crossroads of circumstance, the proving ground of 'What happened? Who's here? Who's coming?' and that is the heart's field."

We enter these memories through our senses, through what we smell, what we see, what we hear. When writing about a place, you can always enter through a sensory door. Annie Dillard's Pulitzer Prize–winning *Pilgrim at Tinker Creek* is one of my favorite books, a master's example of using sensory detail to establish a specific place, though of course it does much more than that.

Another way to enter memory is by saying the name of a place. There's a kind of magic in naming that generalities can't evoke. Tinker Creek, Ghost Ranch, Bean Lake. That last one I'm sure you've never heard of. It's a small lake in Missouri where my family vacationed, where my father could fish and we girls could splash around in the muddy water, getting sunburned and mosquito eaten. I would only have to say "Bean Lake" to my sisters, and their memories would conjure up their own story of our brief carefree time at the lake. My mother had her memories, too, and I doubt the word *carefree* could be found anywhere among them with a husband, three daughters, and a new baby in a rustic fishing cabin with splintering floors, no refrigeration, and little more than a camp stove for preparing meals.

Welty continued, "We do not say simply 'The Hanging Gardens' — that would leave them dangling out of reach and dubious in nature; we say 'The Hanging Gardens of Babylon' and there they are, before our eyes shimmering and garlanded and exactly elevated to the Babylonian measurement."

My Bean Lake is hardly the Hanging Gardens of Babylon, but by saying its name, I am transported back to a time of childhood, and not just to the smell of lake water on sunburned skin or to the taste of cherry Popsicles that barely cleansed the residue of that muddy water from my mouth; the memory is tinted by the color of childhood — in my mind, innocence awash in sepia.

EXPLORATION: Place and Memory

Write the name of a place at the top of a clean sheet of paper. Maybe it's a place you've wanted to write about for some time, or maybe the name came spontaneously. If you're writing fiction, write a place for a scene to unfold, and let the memories be those of your characters.

If this is a place where many memories are rooted, begin by writing some sensory details as they come to you, and as you write them down, the particular memory that wants to be written about will appear almost organically out of the writing, taking its shape from the particular season you've chosen (or that chose you), or from the time of day, or from the sounds that you hear. In this way, you'll go from the generalities of your description to the specifics of the memory.

Where I Come From: The Geography of Home

"My wound is geography. It is also my anchorage, my port of call." So begins Pat Conroy's novel *The Prince of Tides*.

Something happened to my father after he retired. He'd gone back to Missouri for his fiftieth high school reunion, and when he returned to San Diego he wanted to put the house he and my mother had lived in for decades on the market and go back to St. Joseph. Never mind that his children and most of his grandchildren were here or that few of his family or old friends in Missouri were still alive. He wanted to sell it all and move back. "Move back home," he said. There must have been something in the nostalgia of it all, maybe the spirit of the landscape that communicated with him more deeply than Southern California's palm trees and mild weather.

My parents never did leave California, but a few years ago, I, too, found myself nostalgic for my Missouri roots and in a writing practice session wrote the bones of what later became this prose poem.

THE GEOGRAPHY OF HOME

These days, something about your Missouri roots pulls at you. Something deep and deeper yet that you can't explain. That dark earth where corn grows tall and green, where a girl can get lost in the fields. You remember staking tomatoes and the way your daddy taught you the intricacies of the square knot. How, one small hand over the other, you learned — *right over left and under/*

left over right. A litany you still say when you tie back the bougainvillea vines, when you wrap a bow around a gift.

There's no place better for growing peaches. Those boot-heels you can buy at every farmer's stand along the two-lane roads. And cherries and cucumbers and green beans long as your middle finger. Dusty daisies blooming against green ditches and locusts in walnut trees, raising their song in a choir of summer hunger.

You wonder why, after all these years, the geography of home is country highways and gravel roads and farms with ponds where cattle stand, ankle deep in mud. And how the girl who craved California is now the woman who thinks porch swings and ice tea and long twilight evenings when fireflies blink bright as memory. And where listening for the cicada song, you hear someone calling your name.

After this poem was published, I heard from several people who said they, too, had hankerings for their midwestern origins (*hankering* being a quintessential midwestern word). I don't expect I'll pack it all up and move back; among other things, I'm spoiled by the weather in San Diego. Still, there sets upon me sometimes a longing for a home that I can't define and perhaps will never find. This is when I need to breathe in the feeling and go inward to find that homeplace within and where I can be with the feeling and find my inner response. Not "where do I want to live?" but "what is home?"

Edna O'Brien wrote, "It is true that a country encapsulates our childhood and those lanes, byres, fields, flowers, insects, suns, moons and stars are forever re-occurring and tantalizing me with a possibility of a golden key which would lead beyond birth to the roots of one's lineage."

EXPLORATION: The Geography of Home

The place you were born, where you come from, may not be what you call home today, but still, its name, its essence, its spirit was imprinted on your original awareness. You may have left there so young that you're not certain whether the specific details you remember are yours or whether they come from stories you were told.

For this Exploration, use the prompt "I come from..." and freewrite for twenty minutes, more if you want and if the words and memories are still alive. Remember: sensory details and specifics. Write the names of places and things.

Place as Emotional Geography

Place and emotion are intertwined. We remember places because of an emotional connection: this is the place we said good-bye, this is the place I lost my grandmother's ring, this is where I discovered _____. This is the place someone died, someone is buried. This is the place I connected with something greater than myself.

Conservationist Alan Gussow wrote, "The catalyst that converts any physical location — any environment if you will — into a place, is the process of experiencing deeply. A place is a piece of the whole environment that has been claimed by feelings."

Emotions are bound up in place. Sometimes we are able to revisit those places and relive the experience, though when we do, the original feelings are replaced or colored over by new feelings.

On the twenty-fifth anniversary of my husband's death, I drove to the place we'd lived together, the place he died, the place we scattered his ashes. It was a pilgrimage in a way; I hadn't been to our previous home in many, many years and the last time I'd visited, the landscape had much changed. Housing developments claimed the hillsides where there had been open sky. A stoplight replaced the battered stop sign. This time a mall had been erected, and the streets expanded to include left-turn lanes and center islands. I felt like a foreigner.

Much had changed at our old homestead, too. The house was empty, for sale by the bank. The hillsides Tom had planted with a half-dozen species of avocados, scores of young trees he never saw grow to maturity, had been torn away. The orchard where he'd gathered oranges, tangerines, grapefruit, and lemons, using his shirttails as a basket — and where his ashes had been sprinkled — was gone. A single, dying peach tree was all that remained of the place he had planted and nurtured and where he'd felt most at home since leaving Canada decades earlier.

> **NOTES FOR NURTURING WILD VOICE**
>
> - Put a comma instead of a period and go further, deeper.
> - Do something different.
> - Read writers who write in a wild, authentic voice; read them as a writer — notice what they do, how they do it.
> - Hang out with your own tribe.

As I sat on steps that led down to the devastated orchard, feeling devastated myself, a hummingbird flitted near me, close enough that I could hear the thrum of her wings. She air-danced and balanced for brief moments in what was left of a ragged bougainvillea, her ruby throat glowing in the sunlight; then she was gone. I had always said, whenever I spotted Tom in the orchard with his bright shirt, hoe on his shoulder, whistling, that he was like an exotic bird, briefly landed on his migration to the next place. To me the hummingbird was a sign, a talisman. The wreckage I felt inside was replaced by a feeling of gratitude. Lucky me. I had been fortunate enough to be part of his brief sojourn here as he journeyed on his way to somewhere else.

GREYSTONES

Gillian Moss

Wild Women Writing Workshop (2011)

We lived so close to the sea in Greystones that it became a big part of our new lives together to walk at its edge in the dark, stormy, moonlit Irish nights. Walking along above the rocks. Watching. Listening. Smelling the sea. Experiencing the strength of the waves crashing against the rocks, sending white foaming spray up into the air — many times hitting us, thrilling us.

Walking home, the wind pushing us forward from behind. The moon high and bright, lighting our path together.

Rushing to bed in those exciting, passionate early days of marriage, the moon still shining down on us. The ebb and flow of the sea, and us moving with it.

EXPLORATION: Place as Emotional Geography

Place evokes feelings, and feelings evoke place. You may not have revisited a place so filled with emotion as my pilgrimage to my home with Tom in Jamul. Your feeling for a place may still reside in memory, unchanged from when you experienced it.

One of the reasons writers write and readers read is for discovery. You may find, in writing about a place that holds emotional depth, something new about the place, the event, or yourself you didn't know — especially if you allow the writing to come from the deep place where your authentic voice resides.

For this Exploration, write about a place that holds emotional remembrances. In writing such remembrances, it is tempting to let the pen go still and drift into the memory, which is why writing against time can help to keep the hand moving and the memory flowing onto the page. Set your timer for eighteen minutes, and begin writing.

What We Call Home

"England is my home, London specifically," wrote Angie, a participant in a Wild Women writing workshop. "The streets are paved with the history of my heart." But Angie doesn't live in England.

Basia was born in Chicago but never felt it was home. "The first time I came to California when I was twenty-one, I knew I belonged here." "I never felt quite at home growing up in the suburbs, and as soon as I could, I went to live in a gigantic city, thinking this was the solution. For more than a decade, I believed in major cities — until I realized that the connection I was seeking wasn't in other places but in nature," said Midge.

Story after story of women who were born in one place but feel at home in another. It is as if they were zygotes, picked up by the wind and blown willy-nilly to a place utterly unlike what they know in their bones to be Home. I've told my own story of being transplanted from the Midwest to San Diego, where the landscape fits me and where I say my prayers in the language of the sea.

"From the first time I traveled to Maui in 2005, I felt home.

Just the feel of the air is nurturing....I found a poetry group there, a Zen temple and a sweet young priest with whom I meditate, a pine forest above the ocean where I go alone — only the susurration of treetops in the breeze for companionship," said Sylvia.

This inner place is where our soul is nurtured. Where is it for you? A hammock in the backyard, a walk among the trees? I have spoken love words to a stand of eucalyptus trees along a trail in Balboa Park, and said, "Thank you" as I leaned, full-bodied and ten feet up, against the great curving branch of a fig tree in that same park.

Do you paddle a canoe along a river or a stream, kayak in ocean caves, dive below the ocean's skin into the depths of the sea? Do you dance, make art, make noise? Nap in the sunshine like an old cat? Do you drum at sunrise, camp in the woods, or howl under a full moon with only a couple of dogs for company, as Annie did?

MY MOON EXPERIENCE

Annie Kolls

Hot Nights, Wild Women Writing Workshop (1997)

While we caught our breath I sniffed the dogs' muzzles, and blew air out of my nose, just like they did. They sniffed me back. Suddenly I didn't care if the grass was wet. I lay back on it, still looking at the moon. Megan licked my nose and most of one lens of my glasses, which altered my vision in a soft watery way. I closed the "good" eye and studied the moon through the "wolf" saliva. It was beautiful. It wavered in a surreal dance. I took off my glasses and curled up on the grass. The dogs shifted closer and curled up beside me.

No one ever came outside to see what all the howling was about. There was nothing out of the ordinary, really. Just three wolves, sleeping in the moonlight.

How and when do you make time to go Home?

EXPLORATION: The Most Beautiful Place on Earth

In *Desert Solitaire*, Edward Abbey wrote, "Every man, every woman, carries in heart and mind the image of the ideal place, the right place, the one true home, known or unknown, actual or visionary."

Write about your "right place, the one true home, known or unknown, actual or visionary."

Continuing the Journey: Further Explorations into Writing Place

1. Create a narrative guide to notable sites in your life: the ten most romantic settings (and who you were there with), the seven most exciting locations (and what made them so), the eight historic places (and what happened there), the four life-changing crossroads, the six sacred sites. Come up with your own categories.

    Using your narrative guide, select among the sites, and do expanded writings in your notebook.

2. Describe the place where you feel most at home. Write about who you are when you are there, and what is left behind when you leave.

3. Explore the geography of your psyche by reconstructing places you have lived. Make a list of places you've lived.

Name the cities, the neighborhoods, the streets. Write the addresses, if you can remember them, the colors of the buildings and their shapes. Describe the architecture. Describe the homes from inside out, outside in. Choose one place from your list to write about, and as you write, echo the language that was spoken there. Let it come from your wild voice.

4. Geography influences the way we speak and write, the food we eat and how we cook, our values, our cultural awarenesses. Place also influences the music we listen to, the entertainment we experience, the flora and fauna we live with, our prejudices and preferences. We're affected by the weather, the culture, the landscape, the palette of colors and shades and tone, and a myriad of other elements that make up our daily life.

    On a slip of paper, note the different elements you'd like to write about. You can begin with a prompt such as "write about the weather I grew up with" or "this is the soundtrack of my home" or "the view out my bedroom window." Make prompts for food, language, architecture, nature, anything and everything having to do with geography and place that might influence a life, now or in the past. At any given writing practice session, pull one of the strips from its holding place and write for seventeen minutes.

5. When I think of (place), I see _____, or I hear _____, or I smell _____. Write for a few minutes from each sense. Use this Exploration as a practice, first of focusing on one sense, then of integrating the senses together into a whole piece. You'll probably eliminate some in the merging; choose the strongest details,

the most telling, those that most capture your "sense" of the place.

Notes from the Journey

1. Your Journey Notes journal is filling with recordings of your Explorations into your wildish nature. Do you see patterns or cycles in your writing? In reviewing my notebooks, I notice there are certain times in the month when my writing is more creative, looser, and wilder. One of the reasons I suggest dating the page is so that you can track these cycles. Discovering times when wild voice is more present may help you plan writing retreats or, at least, longer periods for writing sessions.

2. Have you, like Annie Kolls, gone outside at night and howled at the moon? Even though he used a male pronoun, we Wild Women should pay heed to Charles Simic, who wrote, "He who cannot howl will not find his pack."

    Most months I make note of the date of the full moon and sometime during the three-day cycle, let loose with a good long howl. Try it. You may feel a little silly or embarrassed, but I bet you'll touch into some wild, too.

3. Did all the writing about place, especially the noting of specifics and the writing through the senses, heighten your awareness of where you are now? It's good to record some of the details you notice each day. This will help you stay grounded in the physical world and also keep your writer's senses alert.

7 LOVES AND LOVERS
Journey into the Heart

The moment I heard my first love story I started looking for you,
not knowing how blind that was.

Lovers don't finally meet somewhere.
They're in each other all along.

— Rumi

Say the word *love* and a hundred thousand angels sing. Say *love* and roses bloom and rivers change their course. Say *love* and one person hears violins, while someone else starts wailing on an old blues harp. Maybe for others it's like what Lily Tomlin said in one of her acts: "If love is the answer, could you please rephrase the question?"

Love love love. This is the stuff of poetry and song, myth and legend. Love opens our eyes and then blinds us. It is both joyous and heartbreaking. It is at once simple and bewildering. When love beckons, we are powerless to resist, and when we are in love it is as if we have transcended Self.

It's easy to get sentimental when writing about love, too, to go all gushy and Hallmark-y. Or to stain purple in our prose with hearts pounding, eyes glistening, lips atremble. We set the stage with candles, soft music; surely there's a full moon.

"Speak to us of love," Almitra said to the Prophet, in Kahlil

Gibran's long prose poem, "and there fell a stillness upon them." So, too, when we try to describe this feeling, this state of being — the giving and receiving — words fail, language becomes inadequate, pens falter.

But still we try. We are on a quest to speak in our wild voice, to write from our authentic wildness, and for now love is both the question and the answer, and we continue on.

When I write about love, I burn a red candle. Red is the traditional color of love — red for hearts, red for passion, red for desire. When I light the candle, I invite all the gods and goddesses of love, all the muses and magi, all the nymphs and fairy folk, and the spirits of the wild to join us for our time together. I will do the same now, as we set forth in our Exploration of love and lovers.

How Does Wild Woman Love?

There is a soul-hunger in us to give and receive love, to be seen as we are, accepted and loved for our authenticity. Maybe we can never be completely seen or understood — this inner/ outer woman we are, both wild and domesticated — but we need a partner up to the challenge of at least trying to understand our wildish nature.

This soul mate may not be our first or only love. Maybe we are lucky in love and have truly loved and been loved more than once. Others of us may never find our true love, by choice or by accident. We may forget to open our eyes and listen to intuition's wisdom. But something within us begins to stir when we are still girls, this kindling of a fire we may spend a lifetime alternately feeding and quenching, stoking and banking.

Why Do Fools Fall in Love?

We fall in love by degrees, and there are as many different kinds of love and falling as there are days in a year. Sometimes we're swept off our feet — the burning bush of love — and sometimes love grows incrementally. Occasionally we get crushes, even if we're with someone else. These little crushes can bring excitement to our lives; maybe we even fantasize about our crush while making love with the one we're with. (There's no wrong in that, but perhaps it's best kept to ourselves.) There are heart throbs and passing fancies, main squeezes (as we used to say) and significant others. True commitments and life partners. And let us not forget unrequited love, foolish love, crazy love, lost love, and deepest soul-mate love.

"And why do people want to be in love?" Susan Sontag asked, then answered her own question. "Partly, they want to be in love the way you want to go on a roller coaster again — even knowing you're going to have your heart broken."

PICTURES IN THE SMOKE

Dorothy Parker

Oh, gallant was the first love, and glittering and fine;
The second love was water, in a clear white cup;
The third love was his, and the fourth mine;
And after that, I get them all mixed up.

EXPLORATION: Loves and Lovers

It's list-making time again. Lists — to-do, shopping, notes-to-self — are a kind of practical shorthand that most of us use every day. However, making an intuitive list, as we've done in previous Explorations, gets the "thinker" out of the way and allows the deeper, more intuitive thoughts to arise. It's here we're given access to material that we mightn't have come up with if we'd tried to think our way into what matters to us. The more we work intuitively, free of conscious purpose, the more meaningful images and impressions come to us. Also, on the practical side, making a list helps us to compile prompts for additional writing sessions. If it shows up on your list, there's likely a story that longs to be told.

And so, we make our list.

Write the name of everyone to whom you have given a piece of your heart, from your first playground crush to your first real love to your current love, which may be the same. If you don't have a current, then list your last and everyone in between. If you can't remember a name, any outstanding feature will do — "that weekend in Big Sur, the guy with the motorcycle and the dog." The names don't have to be in chronological order, either; just write them as they come to you. One may trigger another that has a connection that might not be visible on the surface. Intuition works by association; you can trust it knows what it's doing.

After you've completed the list, take a few moments of quiet. When you're ready, review your list, and when you sense a certain pull at one of the names, open to a fresh page in your notebook for an extended writing about this romance or fling or commitment.

You may want to begin by putting the name at the top of the page and letting images come to you, any one of which can lead into story. Or begin with a specific detail — something physical or a feeling detail: "Every spring I long to return to

Barcelona." Set your timer for seventeen minutes, or simply begin and write as long as the energy flows.

Sometimes when I'm doing timed, focused writing and the time is up but the writing is too hot to quit, I'll set my timer for another seventeen minutes and continue writing. And still again if the urgency to continue persists. This way I sustain the tension and intensity of the timed writing, which for me keeps the pen moving and the ink flowing and me pretty much out of the way.

Complete story collections and memoirs have been written from the perspective of a life of love and lovers. Scheherazade did this in *One Thousand and One Nights*, telling the king love story after love story, thereby saving her life. More recently Jo Ann Beard wrote a memoir titled *The Boys of My Youth*. Pam Houston wrote *Cowboys Are My Weakness*, a story collection, and Gina Frangello a novel, *A Life in Men*. Would a linked story collection or a memoir or a series of poems serve as a way for you to give your wild voice to your love stories? Consider your list again, go on some writing expeditions, and see what might be there.

Lost Love

And then there's the one who broke your heart. The one who left too soon. The one who got away. The one who — how did it happen? A journey, an assignment, took them to another part of the world, or you; a drifting away. The one who died.

WHAT MY LIPS HAVE KISSED
Edna St. Vincent Millay

What lips my lips have kissed, and where, and why,
I have forgotten, and what arms have lain

Under my head till morning; but the rain
Is full of ghosts to-night, that tap and sigh
Upon the glass and listen for reply;
And in my heart there stirs a quiet pain,
For unremembered lads that not again
Will turn to me at midnight with a cry.
Thus in the winter stands the lonely tree,
Nor knows what birds have vanished one by one,
Yet knows its boughs more silent than before:
I cannot say what loves have come and gone;
I only know that summer sang in me
A little while, that in me sings no more.

Write about the one you regret losing.

"Another Somebody
Done Somebody Wrong Song"

What about the one who said, "I'll be back," and never was?
The one who ran off with someone else? The one who done
you wrong? Revenge with a knife or a gun in your hand might
not be your best move, but with your pen — go for it! From
my experience writing with a pack of Wild Women, this topic
is spilling over with thick, rich juice.

Write about the one who done you wrong.

Soul Mates: The Complete Union

Myth, legend, and folk- and fairy tales abound with stories of
soul mates. Osiris and Isis, Psyche and Eros, Midir and Aideen,
whose love cannot be broken, even by the most powerful magic.
Romeo and Juliet. The prince's search for the one whose lovely
foot the glass slipper fits, the perfect kiss that awakens Sleeping
Beauty. All those frogs. No wonder we believe in soul mates.

"For the most part, I don't believe in woo-woo new age stuff, though I have often wished I did," said Drusilla. "But when it comes to the relationship I have with my husband of almost fifty years, I believe there is some alchemy involved, something predestined about our coming together."

An old Chinese folktale, "The Old Man under the Moon," tells of a deity who ties a red string around two people — "the red string of fate" — and once done, their destiny is sealed.

Do you believe in soul mates? Destiny? What does *soul mate* mean to you? Write two pages.

Erotic Love

I once knew a woman who said, "When I fall in love, I fall in love all over my body." And she had plenty of body with which to fall in love. Our bodies are one alive and lovely erogenous zone. Ask anyone who's felt the erotic tension when even the fingers of two people's hands resting on a tabletop yearn toward one other. Remember the thrill of a lover's breath against your hair? The drips of honey, the cool showers; toes. Sexuality, sensuality, and eroticism are vital to our wildish nature. And what a wild adventure it is to write about them. Our bodies may be a temple, but that doesn't mean we can't make our joyous noise — our whoops and hollers, our soft murmurs and moans. Writing about erotic love with a tribe of Wild Women is some of the most playful, liberating, bawdy fun I've had. Here's one sample:

LEFTOVERS

Wild Women Writing Workshop (2006)

You bring lunch, leftovers from Easter dinner. Ham. Asparagus. Sweet potatoes. There must have been stuffed eggs, some hot cross buns. I've hardly wiped my lips or set aside my tray when you pull me to the floor, a little rough, but who cares. It's Easter and we're celebrating miracles.

You rise again.

"The true liberation of eroticism lies in accepting the fact that there are millions of facets to it, a million forms of eroticism, a million objects of it, situations, atmospheres and variations," wrote Anaïs Nin, whose collections of journals, stories, and letters are proof of her beliefs. She continued, "We have, first of all, to dispense with guilt concerning its expansion, then remain open to its surprises, varied expressions."

MOLLY BLOOM'S SOLILOQUY, *ULYSSES*
James Joyce

Yes and how he kissed me under the Moorish wall and I thought well as well him as another and then I asked him with my eyes to ask again yes and then he asked me would I yes to say yes my mountain flower and first I put my arms around him yes and drew him down to me so he could feel my breasts all perfume yes and his heart was going like mad and yes I said yes I will Yes.

EXPLORATION: An Erotic Monologue

A monologue is the voice of one person talking. Here the story is told by the person or character speaking. The audience for this speech may or may not be present — the person or character speaks on the phone, to someone asleep or in another room, or to an imagined someone, maybe someone dead, or in the case of an interior monologue, as in Molly Bloom's, to herself, thinking the words as much as speaking them aloud. A monologue may also speak directly to the reader or to an audience.

For this Exploration, write an erotic monologue. Visualize anticipating an encounter, reliving an encounter, reliving history. Maybe you or your assumed character will voice her attitude about something provocative — food as sensuous, flowers as erotic — anything that will lead into the erogenous, the sensual, the sexy metaphor, or the steamy entendre.

A monologue is most often written in first person ("I"), though second person ("you") is sometimes used.

The Voyeur

Scopophilia, from the Greek, means "love of looking" and refers to the erotic pleasure experienced through viewing. I prefer the less scientific-sounding word *voyeurism* and readily admit to gazing into passing backyards from my perch aboard a train and glancing into lighted windows as I walk my twilit neighborhood. I don't mean I actually go all Peeping Tom and peek into people's windows. My glance reflects more a natural curiosity about witnessing others' intimacies from the distance of the sidewalk — the act of a couple eating a meal together, a hand on a cheek, or a smile that excludes me and everything else in the world. I will confess that once, in the middle of a restless night in Barcelona, I stood at my

> ### NOTES FOR NURTURING WILD VOICE
>
> - Pay attention to nature — the beauty and the violence, the births and the deaths, the life and the destruction of life.
> - Be aware of your animal self.
> - Write naked, and not just metaphorically.

darkened window and watched a couple in the hotel across the street making clumsy love until the scene lost its intimacy and became boring. I'm not much for pornography, but give me an erotic film or artfully lit photographs of curved bodies, and I become a voyeur, delighting in the intimacy of the erotic.

In an interview once, Canadian author Carol Shields said, "The most erotic scene I've ever witnessed was my uncle bending over at the dining room table to kiss the back of my aunt's neck. It was summer time and she was wearing a sundress and just lifting a spoonful of sherbet to her lips. They were middle-aged then. I was a child, maybe nine or ten. But I recognized 'it.' "

The "it" is why we read love stories by writers not afraid of the wild. Why we watch and watch again certain French films and have on our shelves collections of erotic photographs. The "it" is why my mother hid in the bathroom to read *Peyton Place*, and why, as a teenage girl, I dared D. H. Lawrence.

EXPLORATION: Writer as Voyeur

Shields went on, "I thought I might try to write about this experience. But all the old problems occur — how to make such a small moment felt."

For this Exploration, write about lovers you have watched: strangers in a café or restaurant, a twosome in the park or in a car stopped at a light, a couple dancing or kissing, an intimate touch between people.

Write about your experience as voyeur, a description not just of what you witnessed but of your inner response to what you saw. With your careful choice of detail, try to make the moment felt.

Love and Making Love Are Not Always Synonymous

Though in our fantasies we may imagine sensuous beds or lounges, pillows, steaming baths fragrant with oils, secluded pools or soft forest floors, a picnic spread beneath a shady tree, often seduction or love making or sex-on-the-run happens in less romantic, comfortable, or private locations.

Who doesn't remember the steering wheel or gearshift getting in the way; the air mattress that lost its air; the faucet on the kitchen sink and how it nudged the spine. Those cold, hard concrete floors; the broom closet; the bathroom on the 737 on the way to Denver. (Thank you, Erica Jong, for giving us "the zipless fuck" in *Fear of Flying*.) The bugs, the mosquitoes, the sand in uncomfortable locations.

EXPLORATION: Write about a Time You Made Love...

I got the prompts for this Exploration from my friend David Cohen, who has kindly allowed me to use them in my writing workshops. I write each of the prompts on a little slip of paper, which I then fold and put in a container. Then, for the writing session, I have workshop participants pull out a prompt. It's the spontaneity of the prompts that makes them so effective and inspires our wildest, most authentic writing to them; we don't have time to think of what we want to write, we simply respond. As Chögyam Trungpa Rinpoche put it, "First thought, best thought."

Within these prompts may be some you might not want

to write about. Maybe you're embarrassed, or the censor is trampling over what could be a deep and wildish writing time. Or maybe you haven't had an experience with the doings the prompts suggest. Well, then, make it up. Give it to a character. No one says everything we write has to be true. I take that back; it does have to be "true," but it doesn't have to be factual or autobiographical. This is where fiction comes into play.

Here are the prompts. I suggest you do as we do in the workshops. Put them on individual slips of paper and draw one for a spontaneous response.

Write about a time you made love...outside.
Write about a time you made love...passionately.
Write about a time you made love...unexpectedly.
Write about a time you made love...illegally.
Write about a time you made love...slowly.
Write about a time you made love...secretly.
Write about a time you made love...that you're ashamed of.
Write about a time you made love...with someone new.
Write about a time you made love...in a public place.
Write about a time you made love...in a car.
Write about a time you made love...and you didn't want to.
Write about a time you made love...with a stranger.
Write about a time you made love...in the daylight.
Write about a time you made love...in a motel.
Write about a time you made love...in a dream.

Now pull your own slip of paper and write, wildly, spontaneously, for fifteen minutes.

Love and Intimacy

To be loved, to be truly seen by another and to truly see another — this intimacy of two souls, each individual longing to merge, and in the merging, to nourish and transform each other — this is Wild Woman's deep love quest.

"I was initiated into womanhood by the touch of the first lover who was willing to give me voice," wrote Angie, a Wild Woman writing workshop participant. "He touched me naked but not sexual, letting me cry in his arms, watery remembrance of past pain, dripping down his chest in salty rivulets. I was thirty-six and had only ever been mother, maid, whore, and possession. For the first time I was allowed to be a woman, free and wild."

Jennifer wrote of a similar experience: "[My life partner has] really 'seen' me and let me see his appreciation of me, too. That might have been as profound as seeing myself, to experience his acceptance and love of me — physically and emotionally."

Continuing the Journey: Further Explorations into Loves and Lovers

1. As in each of our sessions, we bring with us a token or a talisman or a memento to be our symbol and to inspire us during the writing. Did you find a keepsake that spoke to you of love and lovers? At workshops our altar has contained wedding rings, photographs, love letters, a book of love poems, a rose dipped in lacquer, its edges rimmed in gold, and many other items, each with its own meaning. Write from the talisman you brought; tell its story.

2. Myths, fairy tales, and legends relate stories of love potions and spells and the magical transformations of love. Write about a spell you created or a spell you'd like to create, or a time when you must have fallen under someone's spell for the magical transformation you experienced.

3. Photographs hold stories — not just about the subject matter but about the before and after of the image itself, the occasion of the photograph being taken (is it posed? candid? a happy-snap of a happy time?). There's a story in why you kept it and where you keep it. For this Exploration, look at a photograph of a lover, past or present, alone or with the two of you together, and write the story the photograph holds, or describe the people in the photograph, not just how they appear, but the emotional reading of them you intuitively pick up.

4. The beautiful art book *Love Letters: An Anthology of Passion* begins with this quote, which is tucked inside a tiny envelope on the book's cover: "It is not only necessary to love, it is necessary to say so."

    How long has it been since you've received a love letter? Or written one? It's so easy to talk on the phone, to text, to email, and even to post our love on Facebook. But I'm referring to a real love letter, one you can hold in your hand and read and maybe sigh or smile as you receive the gift of a tender memory?

    For this Exploration, write a love letter. Because it can be a letter you never send, you can write to anyone you love or have loved or have dreamed of loving. The intended recipient doesn't have to be someone you know or even someone who is still alive. Open your wild heart and your imagination, and let your pen lead the way.

5. Among the many anonymous quotes about love is one that compares love to playing the piano: "First you must play by the rules, then you must forget the rules and play from your heart."

List the rules for love and the ways you have kept them
— and broken them.

6. We've written about the ways our heart has been broken,
   but there may have been a time when you broke someone
   else's heart. Stepping back from what the ego might want
   to write, eliminate all judgments and excuses, and write
   the story. One approach might be to tell the story from the
   other person's point of view.

Here are some additional prompts if you'd like to keep
exploring:

"If I loved you..."

Write about love at first sight.

This is what women know about love.

This is what men know about love.

Notes from the Journey

1. Have you confirmed yourself as a regular writing practitioner, writing in your Journey Notes journal every day, or
   at least five days a week? Do you use a time or page con-
   straint for your writing, or do you just let 'er rip and write
   until you stop? Or some of both?

2. Have you taken any of the Explorations from this or any of
   the other sessions and revised or rewritten a piece to shape
   it into something more polished? Have you shared any
   of your writing with another Wild Woman, a member of
   your wildish tribe? Are you considering taking on this next
   step in your writing? I hope you're reading your work out
   loud after completing the exercises, if only to yourself. As

you're reading, do you sense when you've found the sound of your authentic voice?

3. Regarding your body and writing: Were you were aware of your body responding to the writing during any of these Explorations? Sometimes when I write erotica or my writing brushes against the sensuous, I experience a response in my body. It's a good thing to turn yourself on with your own writing, same as it is to allow the tears that naturally form and the laughter that wants to roll out. It means you are completely present with the writing, body and soul.

4. Remember to howl!

8 FRIENDS AND COMPANIONS
Finding Your Tribe

Each friend represents a world in us, a world not possibly born until they arrive.

— Anaïs Nin

A friend once gave me a rock engraved with the words "Leap! and the net will appear." The rock was a hefty one, as large as my open palm, solid and weighty.

That rock said friendship to me in so many ways. The stone itself was made of stuff that doesn't fall apart or melt at the least bit of rain (or tears). The word *Leap!* — how often has it been my friends who encourage me to take a chance, to risk, to push against the bounds, to go for it, whatever "it" might be. And finally, the net — what friendship is and always has been for me. Women, and men, too, but primarily women, have been the soft place I can fall into, the support that has kept me from crashing onto some hard surface, real or ego based, a surround both open enough to let in the light and flexible enough to give but not give way.

Ask any Wild Woman what matters most in her life, and she will most likely put friends right near the top of her list. From our playground beginnings to our lingering final years, it is our friends in whom we discover ourselves, with whom we express ourselves, and by whom we know ourselves, and these indispensable, sometimes closer-than-family friends are most often other women.

Did you know that while still in the womb, girls' brains are formed differently than boys' brains? Well, of course you did. But did you know that one of the differences is that girls develop a strong connection between the amygdala, where our emotions reside, and the cerebral cortex, where we process and articulate feelings? Boys have a different physiological connection; they can't access emotional memories or process emotions as easily as girls. You knew this, too. But the point I want to make is that all this linking and connecting has to do with empathy and communication with others, with social functioning, and resolving conflicts — qualities that enhance relationships with others and lead naturally to developing and nurturing friendships.

Of course, we Wild Women don't need scientific data to tell us the value of having friends and the transformative power of friendships. We've known it since we first sought out and found others in the wonder-filled world of the Wild Child. Still, I did come across some interesting studies about women and friendships.

For instance, in what's called the landmark UCLA study, researchers discovered that in addition to the fight-or-flight hormones released in both men and women who are under stress, women also produce the calming hormone oxytocin, which encourages them to "tend and befriend." Here's how it works. Imagine we're prehistoric men and women and the great woolly beast comes growling outside our cave entrance. The men either grab up their clubs and fight the beast or run like hell. Women, on the other hand, gather the children, find one another and, together, plan ways to survive the situation.

Another study indicated that women with friends are less likely to develop physical impairments as they age; the more friends we have the healthier we'll be. Further, women who have friends will probably outlive those who don't, and in the face of loss, when we share the pain and are comforted and supported by our friends, we function better than those who have to go it alone.

All this is to say that women are hardwired or hormoned or programmed to create friendships. We get a kind of natural high when we're in one another's company, which probably accounts for all that laughter you hear whenever any group of Wild Women gets together.

Childhood Friends:
Wild Companions and Adolescent Cohorts

When we were young girls living in a small town in northwest Missouri, my sister and I were friends with a pair of sisters, both the same age as each of us and both with the same first names as ours. While all these decades later my sister remains friends with the sister who has the same name as she, I lost touch with my same-named friend shortly after we moved to California.

My father also kept friends from his long-ago youth right up to the end of his life. Drusilla counts among her closest friends women she's known since elementary school. Comparatively, Dru and my twenty-five-year friendship is still in its early stages.

What is that spark that ignites between two people and remains bright, though time and distance may separate them?

SULA

Toni Morrison

For it was in dream that the two girls had first met. Long before Edna Finch's Mellow House opened, even before they marched through the chocolate halls of Garfield Primary School out onto the playground and stood facing each other through the ropes of the one vacant swing ("Go on." "No. You go."), they had already made each other's acquaintance in the delirium of their noon dreams.

Even though I may not have kept these early friendships, I certainly have the memories, some of them as bright as those summer days when we spread our towels out on the hot sand at Mission Beach and listened to Elvis and the Everly Brothers on our transistor radios, believing that every word they sang was meant for us.

EXPLORATION: Friends from Back When

One of the many ways to use the "I remember..." prompt is to add a name and let memories of that person begin to unspool. At the top of a clean sheet of paper, put "I remember _____" and the specific name of a person you want to direct your memory toward; then write a pageful of two- or three-sentence memories about that person, just enough detail to bring the memory to life. Skip a line between each individual memory until you've written four or five separate incidents or images.

This exercise can build a series of memory threads that may be woven together to create a longer piece (sometimes the intuitive mind will hook memories together in a way that may not be obvious at first read-through), or the individual memories may each be the seed of a separate story.

Another way to access memories or stories from times gone by is to begin with a specific year. Many childhood memories flare when we put ourselves back in the classroom, so try beginning with a school year: "When I was in fourth grade..." An even more direct approach is to begin with a particular season of a specific year. The seasonal aspect will offer up sensory details that make a memory more vivid. For some reason, many of my memories of childhood and adolescence take place in summer.

IN AUGUST WHEN THE GRAPES RIPEN

In August the grapes hung heavy in the arbor, deep purple and glowing among leaves the color of moss and as large as my hand. The arbor, with its sturdy pillars and white wooden benches, ran half the length of the side yard of my best friend's home. Those hot afternoons when the air grew thick with humidity and the winey scent of ripening grapes drove the bees into a frenzy, we'd take our chilled Cokes and fan magazines into the arbor as though we were entering someplace holy.

Remember, in this Exploration you're focusing on friends or experiences with friends rather than on random memories of the time.

Try writing your Explorations in first person, present tense, as if you're still in that particular place at that particular time, and then, in another Exploration, use the reminiscent narrator's voice, as I have done in the previous example, and write in past tense (still in first person), as an adult, looking back and remembering. Either POV (point of view) will accommodate your wild voice.

The present tense may bring alive details you don't consciously remember and lend a lively immediacy to the writing, while the past-tense reminiscent narrator's voice may reveal how the incident affected you and the person you are now. This is often the memoirist's voice.

Stages-of-Life Friendships

We leave high school, we leave home, and sometimes we move far away to attend college, where we form new friendships. Maybe we keep one or two of our closest high school friends, but the others drift away.

After college, when we go solo into the larger world, we leave most of our college friends behind, too, and new friendships develop through our jobs or through activities with other young singles.

When and if we marry or form partnerships, each of us brings friends into the mix, and friendships take the form of couples. If we have children, our friends are other young mothers with whom we now have so much in common. Then, as the children grow and we become "chauffeurs" and team mothers, our friendships take root in the grassy fields of baseball diamonds, in carpools, or in Scouts meetings. But the friendships that formed around the kids' activities often fade away once the kids leave home. And so it goes.

As the saying has it, "bloom where you are planted"; friendships flower with people we meet and interact with in our daily lives. We befriend the women with whom we run or share a yoga or meditation practice. The places we've lived, clubs we belong to, church groups, study groups, spiritual groups, writing groups — in every aspect and at every stage of our lives we make friends.

But trying to maintain all these friendships over the years is like trying to hold air in a net: impossible. As our lives and needs and interests change, our friendships fluctuate. I can't even remember the names of some of the women I was close to when my son played whatever sport the season dictated, nor, I expect, do they remember me. But at the time we saw each other several times a week at Pop Warner or Little League or basketball or swimming, cheering the team and sharing our secrets in equal measure. All these years later, I don't even remember the secrets.

EXPLORATION: It Was a Time When...

I am imagining a list of "times when" and "friends who." This collection could go on for pages, whole notebooks of "times when" and "friends who." And what a wealth of stories could come from that. Each friendship is a journey in its own right, and each group of friends provides traveling companions along the way.

Some friends we might have difficulty remembering, until we begin to piece together a description.

TORCH SONG

Katie Roiphe

My memory of Stella, at nineteen, is neither as crisp nor as detailed as it should be. It's only with a tremendous effort of will that I can bring her into focus at all. She is wearing a complicated black outfit that looks likes rags pinned together with safety pins, and black stockings, with deliberate runs laddering her legs.

And some we might have recognized right away as special, as someone we wanted to know better.

DIARY

Virginia Woolf

Monday 15 September

Vita was here for Sunday, gliding down the village in her large new blue Austin car, which she manages consummately. She was dressed in ringed yellow jersey, and large hat, and had a dressing case all full of silver and night gowns wrapped in tissue.... Oh yes, I like her; could tack her on to my equipage for all time; and suppose if life allowed, this might be a friendship of a sort.

For this Exploration, think of a time and of a friend. Write a description of a friend you remember or of something you experienced together.

Something that helps me when I'm beginning a scene is to write, at the top of the page, the place where the scene will happen. I make a note of some sensory details: whether it's night or day, a brush stroke of what the place looks like or smells like, if there are any sounds (there always are), who's involved, and maybe something of the emotional tenor if I know what the scene is about. All this detailing at the beginning brings me present in a place and time and with those who are involved. After I'm done making all these notes, I begin with one of the sensory details, then let the scene roll out as it will. Try it and see if it works for you.

Make a special place in your Journey Notes for a section on "A time when, and a friend who" so you can continue to explore friendships past and present, short-lived and long-term.

EXPLORATION: Friendships Lost

Angie from a past Wild Women writing workshop wrote, "I had a group of women whom I could count on to be available on a Saturday night to go be girls. We could go to the shooting range or to the piano bar to sing at the top of our lungs to bawdy songs while eating junk food and tossing back beers. I could invite them over for pedicures and gossip or play board games with them until the wee hours of the morning. Nothing I ever said or did was judged and there were always an adequate number of shoulders to cry on. Even if they didn't agree with me, they had my back."

And then she moved from California to Arkansas, where, she reported, "I am quite solitary."

After a move or the break-up of a marriage or partnership, the loss of friendship is often part of the debris. Often our interests naturally change, and we leave friendships behind. Sometimes we lose our friends under the most difficult and painful circumstances — illness or death.

This Exploration invites us to write about the loss of these friends, some of whom were quite close, but... , or until...

Write about the loss.

Another approach: Because it has the built-in tension that makes for good storytelling, an especially evocative approach might be "The Friend Who Got Away," the story of a friendship that didn't just fade away or was lost to illness or death, but one that was deliberately broken.

Who was it, and what happened?

Friends No Matter What or Where: BFFs

The list is long: Hermia and Helena in *Midsummer Night's Dream*, Charlotte and Elizabeth in *Pride and Prejudice*, Celie and Shug in *The Color Purple*, Lucy and Ethel, Mary and Rhoda, Carrie and Charlotte and Miranda and Samantha. We could go on and on naming best friends in literature, film, TV, and popular culture: such is the appeal of stories of the close and enduring friendships of girls and women.

These days they're called BFFs or "besties." Those in-it-for-the-long-haul, call-at-3:00-AM, call-*no-matter-what* friends on whom we depend for companionship and support, whose opinion we value above all others, who teach us about ourselves and with whom we can absolutely be our most authentic and wild selves.

These are the friends we trust utterly, with whom we cry and laugh (oh, yes, the laughing), and with whom we communicate more deeply and honestly than with any other. They are our soul sisters and sometimes our saviors.

Nicole wrote this about her best friends: "Girlfriends who knew me at my worst and who love me anyway. The friends who risk telling you what you don't want to hear. I see them so rarely now, but love them with a deep ferocity time and distance don't change. Can one truly be 'best friends' with someone they speak with every two years? Every five? Yes."

And is it possible to have more than one best friend? Yes. I know; I have three, and I feel wealthy in these friendships and grateful beyond words.

EXPLORATION: Best Friends

Scene one: Last year a Facebook friend posted a long-ago picture of me posed in my flannel nightgown sitting beside a

Christmas tree; I am eleven or twelve. The photo carries the handwritten caption "Betty's best girl friend."

Scene two: As I wrote this chapter, I brought to my writing table a photo album from a late-eighties adventure my daughter and I took to Europe. In the album are pictures of our time in Paris, where we rendezvoused with my bestie Camille.

Two different best friends, friendships decades apart, one that lasted a few short adolescent years, the other nearly thirty years in the making and still vibrant and wild.

Write about your best friends. Use photographs to spark memories, or simply begin with a prompt, like the line from the song, "People, let me tell you 'bout my best friend..."

Another Exploration: I once wrote a letter to my then–best friend Bonnie on a roll of toilet paper and sent it to her in Los Angeles, where she was spending a few weeks with her father. We don't write hand-written letters much anymore, but I still go to my mailbox every day with a certain anticipation — maybe today there will be something special.

Write a letter to your best friend. When we write letters, especially letters to close friends, our most authentic voice is often the one that speaks.

Continuing the Journey:
Further Explorations into Friends and Companions

1. As a child, I never had an imaginary friend, and I've always envied people who did. That may be why I once wrote a story about a kid who was the imaginary friend of a lonely little girl. Psychologists might tell us imaginary friends are the product of creative, curious children who're just trying to figure out the confusing ways of the larger world, but I like to think of it as a kind of enchantment.

Did you have an imaginary friend? Was it another Wild Child?

2. Some say writers speak of their characters as if they're real, and I'll confess to talking about Louise and Sarita as if they live in the same world as the rest of us. I no more want to cause them trouble than I do my "real" friends, although I know I must if the story is to be at all interesting.

Maybe in some ways our characters play the same role as the imaginary friends we had as kids. Or they take on traits we'd like to have in a friend. If I were still a drinker, I can't think of who I'd rather throw back a few shots of Wild Turkey with than my character Ruby Diamond; she could teach me a few things about taking on reality in reality's terms.

Have you written characters who are as alive to you as real friends?

3. Though it's a huge generalization, it's been said that the difference between men and women's friendships is like the "do-be-do-be-do" song. Men do things together; women just like to be together. So how do you view friendships between men and women? Do we do or do we be? Or some of each?

Explore your friendships with men, in general and in particular.

4. Though most friendships develop over a slow dance of disclosure, some rare friendships happen like that trippy, ecstatic kind of falling in love that begins suddenly and feels so right. You meet a woman in a writing class, and you just know you're going to be friends; you see someone at a party and you simply must go up and introduce yourself. Call it the "click" factor — these are women you

immediately realize you want to know better. Sometimes you sense you already do know each other, deeply and well. That's how I felt when I met Camille, even though there's an age difference between us of seventeen years. It may be some kind of psychic connection, the intuition of one person humming a melody and the intuition of the other already knowing the words.

When you write this Exploration, let your memory and your pen linger in the early stages of the friendship, before you had a mutual history.

Try this Exploration another way: Have you met someone you thought you'd be instant and close friends with, only to discover it wasn't to be? Were you disappointed or relieved?

5. I believe that if they thought it worthy, a community of women could find the power to slow the rotation of the Earth and alter the alignment of the heavens. Or maybe that's just how it feels to me when I am in the company of a group of risk-taking, truth-telling, open-hearted, creative, supportive, and authentic women.

My community of women friends is where I go for voice lessons. This is who I want to be with to explore dangerous territory. Here's where wounded self-confidence is tended and tender hearts are cared for. And sometimes we just laugh, and that's enough.

Are you part of a community of women that encourages and nurtures your wild nature?

Notes from the Journey

1. Sometimes doing the day-in and day-out writing in my journal, I find that I'm not really present with my writing

or myself; I'm just filling the pages. No wild voice here. Wake up! I tell myself. Be present!

Has this happened to you as you write your daily Journey Notes? If so, how do you bring yourself back to the present and call up your wild voice?

2. I had a difficult time deciding what to bring to my table to represent friendship as I began writing this chapter. I finally chose the photo album with the pictures of my daughter, my pal Camille, and me. But as I glanced around the room, I saw so many other items that speak of friendship: the old brass calendar Zoe gave me; the glass paperweight, golden as the Barcelona sun, from Diane; the colorful horse figure Carol got for me during our writing retreat in Colorado. Of course, the polished stones from Anita are here; they've been present during all the writing times, and lately, I've added a sprig of sage harvested at Jill's ranch.

> **NOTES FOR NURTURING WILD VOICE**
>
> • Write by hand if you always write on the computer; if you can't write by hand, turn off your computer screen or monitor as you write.
> • Show your work to another Wild Woman writer whom you trust.
> • Surprise yourself.

What have you brought to your writing place to say "friendship?"

3. We all need that balance between solitude and being with others. I'm an extrovert, so I need more time with my Wild Women friends than some of the more introverted members of my pack do. I'm grateful to these quieter women for reminding me of the necessity and the beauty of solitude. What are you grateful to your friends for today?

9 ARTIST/CREATOR
Authentic Expressions
of Wild Woman

The call to create is a calling like no other, a voice within that
howls for expression, shadow longing to merge with light.

— Jan Phillips

Several years ago I was asked to give a talk about women in the arts in celebration of International Women's Day. Whew! I thought, Where do I start? And then I thought, Where do I end? Women and art have existed from the beginning of time and, as long as there is time and there are women, they always will.

When I asked the host how long I had to speak, she said about twenty minutes, "and that includes questions and answers."

Wow! I thought this time. Twenty minutes to talk about the history of the world from the perspective of women in the arts. I could just stand at the podium and say the names of women artists and fill the afternoon. I could fill the day, right on up to dinner. I could lose my voice just saying the names of women in the arts. We could have a filibuster, a marathon, a name-saying, celebration-making, piece of art itself, just naming the women we know who have created — who are creating — art.

And what about the women the world doesn't know? The ones maybe like you and me, like my mother and your mother,

and our aunts and sisters and daughters and nieces, our grandmothers — women who go through their days making art
with nobody knowing our names. Wild Women, all of us. I
like what Virginia Woolf said: "I would venture to guess that
Anon, who wrote so many poems without signing them, was
often a woman."

Claiming Ourselves as Artist/Creator

I recently came across a quote in *Courage to Change* about the
silkworm, which is not a beautiful creature. The quote I read
described the silkworm as "fat and greedy." But, the piece said,
"out of their own substance, they create something beautiful.
They have no choice in the matter. They were born to express
this beauty."

We Wild Women are like the silkworm, not the "fat and
greedy" part but the fact that we can't help but make art.

"Creativity is the work of the heart, unrelated to the econ-
omy of our ordinary lives," said Jan Phillips in her inspiring
book *Marry Your Muse*. "It is not about ego, not about money
or success or failure. It is a calling from the spirit."

And yet through the years, until at least the revolution-
ary sixties, when we began to make some serious noise about
it, women were not encouraged to make art or to celebrate
and express their creativity — at least not much past the age
of seven or eight, when they took away our finger paints and
crayon boxes and told us it was time to get serious.

"Take typing," my mother advised, "then you'll always
have something to fall back on." What she meant, of course,
was that if my marriage didn't work out, I could always be
someone's secretary. I'm not sure what advice mothers give
their daughters these days, but I bet it's not, "Take art, darling.

You'll be adding beauty to the world and expressing your wild, creative nature."

You may have heard something like my mother's counsel, too. Practical, yes, but what a shame that for many of us the practicality wasn't balanced with the encouragement to express our authentic creativity. Instead we heard, "Stay in the lines" or "Polar bears can't live in the jungle." And little by little our wild, intuitive voice was tempered as we learned the rules. "Quit daydreaming," we were told, when daydreaming is the very thing creative minds need.

Claiming ourselves as artist/creator is the same as claiming ourselves as Wild Women. To be wild is to be responsive; to be responsive is to be creative. Though we may hesitate to call ourselves artists, we can't deny we are creative. Creativity is a natural part of all human beings, like love and hope, and even though we may turn away or try to shut it down or deny it, it remains steadfastly within us. We should all be like Janie Crawford in Zora Neale Hurston's novel *Their Eyes Were Watching God*, who "had found a jewel down inside herself and she had wanted to walk where people could see her and gleam it around."

But whether or not we acknowledge ourselves as artists, our creativity leaks out in some manner. For some of us it's the way we prepare and serve meals; for others it's the way we remodel our kitchens. Throw a party, paint a wall, knit a scarf. Open a business, write a proposal, write a poem. Take a photo, take a trip, give a handmade gift.

"There are many expressions of creativity; most are not recognized as art and yet they are. In each of us there is a poet or artist who takes pleasure in making something beautiful or expresses something that is truly us," writes Jean Shinoda Bolen.

This is what I know about creativity: the more you live it, the more whole you feel. The less you judge it, the more pleasure you derive. Creativity brings a wild playfulness to our lives that is often sorely lacking.

EXPLORATION: A Map of Creative Expressions

Remember when you were five years old and didn't know you "couldn't" sing? (I write this for me, the girl who dreamed of growing up to be a singer, the one who couldn't carry a tune even if she had a peach basket.) Remember when you were given paints and a piece of paper and you just sat right down and made a picture? And you liked it. You liked the doing of it, and you liked the picture you created as well. You gave it away as a gift and felt good doing that, too.

For this Exploration, let's make a map. Instead of just listing specific creative expressions, throw words describing them all over the page. Use different-colored pens; make a map bright with wild statements, words, or images. Remember, we're not talking Art, with a capital *A* here; we're talking creative expressions that brought pleasure, that were fun to do or to make. Start with the first thing you remember — whether it's from when you were a child or something you did two days ago — and then fling the memories down in phrases as they come to you.

Here's a partial list, which I translated from my map:

When I pretended I could play the ukulele
The time I roller-skated like a dancer to "Lean on Me"

The collage I made at the women's retreat
Writing about my father and me looking at our big green
     atlas
Dancing the two-step with R. on the cruise
Painting my bedroom walls cranberry
Creating altars for the Wild Women writing workshops

Include at least fifteen or twenty instances when you felt good in the process of being creative. This map making, like any other form of creativity, will become more fluid if you don't try to think of the "right" expression but instead are open to any expression. Don't judge. Just remember, write it down, and celebrate your wild, creative nature.

What to do with the map after you've finished? First of all, keep it close by so you can add to it. The more you see on your map, and the more varied the statements are, the more you may realize what a creative individual you are. There is no one else in all creation like you. Think of that!

As you glance over your map, the idea may come to you of writing a personal narrative essay about a particular experience, what you discovered about yourself or the world and how it changed you. Or maybe the list itself has the makings of a story or a poem. Creating the map might remind you of some creative activity or expression you loved but haven't given much time to lately. Maybe the time to take it up again is now.

"My first felony — I took up with Poetry," wrote Wild Woman Sandra Cisneros. We are creative outlaws, all of us.

Art as Transformation

I was in kindergarten, and our class and all the other elementary school students were sitting cross-legged on the polished hardwood floor of the cafeteria/auditorium for the performance of *Aladdin and His Magic Lantern* by a visiting high school troupe. Never before, in all the books that had been read to me, in all the stories I'd been told, in all the dramas played out on records or on the radio, never before had I experienced such magic. Before me, and me alone, because now all the other students had faded away, appeared mysterious tents draped with brilliant fabrics and furnished with satin pillows as large as my father's easy chair. The play began, and actors adorned in colorful costumes and tasseled shoes with turned-up toes performed their roles. And there was the gleaming magic lantern itself — pure gold, I was certain. Then suddenly a loud drum sounded, and out of a cloud of smoke appeared the genie! ready to grant any wish Aladdin might desire. My wish: that this could go on forever.

This was the first but not the only time I was transformed by a theatrical performance. Nor is theater the only art that has this powerful effect on me. Music, dance, art installations, paintings, films, books, and poetry: I witness art and through my witnessing I am a participant in the making of art — a busker performing in the park where I stop and watch and put my dollar in her basket, a poet reading her work who hears my holy silence at the end of her poem, the man on the banks of the Mississippi River who invited me to look at the moon through his telescope.

"Creativity is interactive and art is alchemical," said Jean Shinoda Bolen in her essay. "Its power is in its capacity to affect and transform the artist and the audience."

Listen to how these Wild Women relate their experiences being transformed by art:

"We were in the Louvre in Paris," said Angie. "As we came down a low staircase from one of the open galleries, there in front of me on a five-foot concrete pedestal, so that she stood above the crowds, was *Winged Victory of Samothrace*. She soared above the crowd breathing liberty to me.... I stood before her in tears, the crowd surging, and me lost in her presence."

"I was crazy-lucky to hear Claudio Abbado conduct Anton Bruckner's Symphony no. 9 at the Lucerne Summer Music Festival," wrote Gina. "At one point the symphony struck such deep chords of resonance in my being that I was crying and shaking. The sound waves in the concert hall seemed to dissolve the boundaries of my skin and bones, erasing any delineation between me and the music, allowing me to merge with its expression of sheer beauty and joy."

Such experiences have a mystical effect; we're changed in a deep, soulful way that inwardly has no language and outwardly often expresses itself in tears.

But it isn't only in grand, sacred places that this magic happens. "Art transformed me in a pigpen," said Anitra. "I was on my knees in the mud and pig shit when I noticed that my body had left and I was purely an eye looking through my camera lens."

> ### NOTES FOR NURTURING WILD VOICE
>
> - It's okay to not know where you're going.
> - It's okay to not know how to get there, even when you think you know where you're going.
> - Don't be afraid to make mistakes.

And sometimes witnessing another's artful expression inspires us to create our own. "That mosaic table I saw twenty years ago in a gallery transformed my life," said Jill. "I dreamed about it all night, bought it in the morning, and have been creating my own mosaics ever since."

Sylvia related, "On a certain day in 1991, I had an encounter with a monarch butterfly and my first poem appeared to me.

That was the beginning of, so far, twenty-two years of writing poetry...and eventually being able to call myself 'a poet.'"

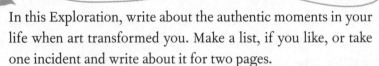

EXPLORATION: Art and Transformation

In this Exploration, write about the authentic moments in your life when art transformed you. Make a list, if you like, or take one incident and write about it for two pages.

Remember to use concrete words. Or if you do use an abstract word such as *beautiful* or *wonderful*, *show* what is beautiful or wonderful to you. Abstract words make the reader guess what you mean; they call for judgments. My "beautiful" and your "beautiful" may be very different. Write in specifics, not generalities; write the names of things. Go for the details.

Your Creative Process

Ah, we creatives are a quirky lot. We have all these habits and perform all these rituals, often without thought, but other times we swear that they are invocations to the muse and that we couldn't possibly do our work unless we first (fill in the blank). It's said that Colette picked fleas from her cat before she settled into her writing, that Baudelaire kept a bat in a cage on his writing desk, and that Henrik Ibsen kept a pet scorpion on his. I've readily admitted to my light-a-candle routine, which is only the first of the rituals I perform, and here I sit at my candle-lit table with all my polished stones.

Artist and writer SARK said, "Your creativity in action is so needed by the world and the people in it. No other person has your eccentric blend of ideas, attitudes, and perceptions."

I love that "succulent wild woman" SARK used the word

eccentric to describe us. *Eccentric* is generally thought of as a polite word for describing someone whom we think of as a little crazy. An "eccentric" is slightly odd, maybe not necessarily dangerous but, "you know," they say, and roll their eyes. To be eccentric is to risk disapproval. In this sense, making art is dangerous.

"I've been absolutely terrified every moment of my life," Georgia O'Keeffe purportedly said, "and I've never let it keep me from doing a single thing I wanted to do."

Making any kind of art takes courage. And so it is no wonder that we have our quirks and idiosyncrasies. These rituals are calming for us, touchstones that both ground us as we begin the creative process and at the same time allow us to leave the safe place of "normal" and enter into the unknown, where anything can happen.

I asked Barbara to describe the feeling and tone of the process of making her art. "Fear and anxiety," she said, "because my mind is all about having to do something purposeful, great and [I] fear failure." But like O'Keeffe, Barbara said she does it anyhow. "Once I'm in it there is a sense of spaciousness — my world expands because my mind follows my heart."

"There really is such a thing as being in 'the flow,' submerging in the work/play of creating that does away with concerns about results and shuts up the critic so that I can enjoy the process," said Lavina, who both paints and writes.

"I've come to accept the friction of frustration as a prerequisite for creation," said Carol. "Once I have successfully started a project, the frustration gives way to deep concentration that takes me out of any self-consciousness. In the groove!"

Maybe you've had the kind of experience that Barbara, Lavina, and Carol speak of. I sure have. When I'm in the process and have surrendered to the work, I am unaware of time passing, of the outside world. Athletes call it being in the "zone" (and by the way, some of them heed some pretty quirky rituals, too, before they enter the playing field). In writing about creativity, Mihaly Csikszentmihalyi coined the now-common term *being in the flow*. Eckhart Tolle and other spiritual teachers call it the ever-present Now. For me, it occurs when I am totally present, aware, and focused and there is no strain, no trying. It is simply doing/being. Sometimes I get so caught up in the fluidity of the process that I can hardly keep up with the next word or shape or image or color; at other times it's like a lazy river, just rolling along, easy as a summer day. I am at one, at peace. I am enough. More than enough: abundant.

And this, I think, this sense of Yes!, this sense of being at one with ourselves during the creative process, is an authentic expression of our natural wildness.

In *Fearless Creating*, creativity coach Eric Maisel wrote, "This wildness has many faces. It is an amalgam of passion, vitality, rebelliousness, nonconformity, freedom from inhibitions. Think of this wildness," he said, "as 'working naked.'"

EXPLORATION: Making Art/Working Naked

How do you express your natural wildness? How do you create? Do you make art or write or spend creative time as part of your daily life? What is your creative process? What rewards and gifts do you receive? And what is their price? That is, do you have to give up something to receive these gifts?

Imagine that you are writing an essay or an article for a publication or for submitting to an anthology on the theme of

creativity. How would you write about your creative process?
Write two pages — more if the piece wants to go on.

Nurturing Your Artist/Creator

When we are at one with our creativity, and by that I mean with
our responsiveness to the world, we are at our most authentic.
It is pointless to say, "I am not creative." If you are alive, you
are creative. Consider it a gift you've been given by a generous
and loving creator. Consider it a fact of your being, the same as
the color of your eyes or the shape of your feet. But unlike your
eye color or the structure of your feet, your creative beingness
is active, alive, a vital force that can change the world. In your
authentic wildness, you are a creative force!

I've told the story for years of how my grandmother said
that when we're born, God puts a thumb right in the center
of our foreheads, imprinting us with our special gift, and says,
"You'll be an actress" or "You'll be a dancer" or "You. You'll
be a writer." I'm not sure if my grandmother really said this or
if I made it up, but I know I believe the fact of it — that we're
all given special gifts that we bring into the world. I also believe
that we have a responsibility to use these gifts, and that if each
of us honors the responsibility and uses the gift, the whole of
humankind will be lifted to a higher plane.

It's not always easy to live up to this responsibility. The
world echoes with the sigh of "not enough time." But if we are
to live an authentic life, if we are to keep our wildish nature
healthy, if we are to experience *all* our joy, we must take care to
protect our creative time and nurture our creative souls.

One year, instead of making New Year's resolutions, I created a list of intentions and sent them out to whatever benevolent presence might be listening. These spoke to my desire to

honor the gift of creativity that I'd been given and to keep it alive in my daily life:

- To honor my creative urges and listen to my deepest longings.
- To be open to wild imaginings and receptive to the charm of the ordinary.
- To keep a place prepared for the muse and to be present so she will know where to find me.
- To find courage to write what wants to be written and patience to give whatever time is needed to write it.
- To acknowledge that what I create is a way of giving back to the Universe.

EXPLORATION: Nourishing Your Artist/Creator

Claiming your authentic wildness through a conscious action each day is a way to give nourishment to your soul. My List of Intentions is another. Scores of books, blogs, newsletters, and creativity coaches offer even more ideas for living a creative, authentic life.

For this Exploration, create your own set of intentions or guidelines to nourish your artist/creator. You may want to develop your own Artist's Creed, as Jan Phillips did in *Marry Your Muse*, or write an Artist's Prayer, as Julia Cameron did in *The Artist's Way*. In *Women Who Run with the Wolves*, Clarissa Pinkola Estés provided a list of ways of "Taking Back the River."

After you've completed your notions of how to nourish your artist/creator, print them out and post them where you'll see them every day. Create a collage or vision board that incorporates your vision. Read your ideas aloud every day to remind yourself what a precious and powerful creative being you are.

Continuing the Journey:
Further Explorations into Artist/Creator

1. Write your autobiography through your creative expressions. You can begin by making stepping-stones of instances or moments or physical manifestations of your creativity, listing them as they come to you, and then creating a chronology from which you write a narrative.

2. Each of us needs a sacred place for our work. The "Maps for the Journey" chapter suggests creating such a space of your own. For this Exploration describe the place you created. If you have in mind a more ideal space, describe what it would look like, what furnishings you would have there, where it would be situated. Write your dream; this is how we begin to manifest.

3. Eleanor Roosevelt told us we must do the one thing we think we cannot do. From the perspective of Wild Woman as artist/creator, what have you done that you thought you couldn't do? What would you still like to do?

4. Write about something you created. Write the story of its birth.

5. In *My Wicked, Wicked Ways*, Sandra Cisneros wrote:

> I chucked the life
> my father'd plucked for me.
> Leapt into the salamander fire.
> A girl who'd never roamed
> beyond her father's rooster eye.

Winched the door with poetry and fled.
For good. And grieved I'd gone
when I was so alone.

Write what you gave up for art.

6. In *A Writer's Book of Days*, I created a list of "Ten Daily
    Habits that Make a Good Writer." One of the habits, which
    isn't just for writers but for all creatives, is to "cross-fertil-
    ize." By that I mean we need to experience other art forms
    to stimulate our own.

    Each day, bring some expression of art into your world.
    It may be as simple as keeping an art book open near your
    desk or listening to music as you work. Take time to visit a
    local gallery, notice the art on the café walls, have lunch in a
    sculpture garden. A busker in the park, a kids' puppet show,
    even a drop-in at a flower shop or an open mic poetry night
    could be just the thing to evoke your own artist or dancer
    or poet. Doing creative work empties us; this is how you fill
    up again. Go!

Notes from the Journey

1. Have you found a way to keep all the lists and prompts from
    the various Explorations in each chapter alive and interac-
    tive as you continue filling your Journey Notes with new
    writing? Some of my notebooks look like they're wearing
    a goofy party hat with all the colored tabs poking out the
    top. Lately I've taken to writing brief notations on the tabs
    so I know why I marked the place. This is much easier than
    thumbing through all of them every time I'm looking for
    something.

2. How did you claim your authentic wildness during this past session? Have you found it difficult to give authentic expression each day? Or has it brought you joy? Have you found a deeper understanding of some of your needs or wants with these regular check-ins? Have you added more ways to make the claim, discarded others?

3. Did you remember to bring a token for your table or altar that represents you as artist/creator — something you created or that speaks of your creativity? My memento as I wrote this chapter was a copy of the chapbook I created from the 2006 Wild Women Writing Workshop. Somewhere I'd found a rolling rubber stamp of animal footprints that I imprinted throughout the booklet. This brought a smile as I remembered our Wild Women footprints being made all over clean, blank sheets of paper.

10 LIFE JOURNEYS
Adventures, Explorations, Quests, and Pilgrimages

Travel is more than the seeing of sights; it is a change that goes on, deep and permanent, in the ideas of living.

— Miriam Beard

Adventure, exploration, journey, odyssey, pilgrimage, quest, sojourn, ramble. Wanderer, vagabond, wayfarer…

Such lovely words that set up a longing in me to move, to go, to pack my bag and hit the road. I am reminded of Elizabeth Gilbert who, in *Eat, Pray, Love*, wrote of the time in Rome when a young Australian girl who was backpacking through Europe asked directions to the train station.

"She was heading up to Slovenia, just to check it out," Gilbert wrote. "When I heard her plans, I was stricken with such a dumb spasm of jealousy, thinking, I want to go to Slovenia! How come I never get to travel anywhere?"

There was Gilbert, living in Italy, just a few months into her yearlong sojourn to Italy, India, and Bali, hungering to get on the road to someplace else. And here I am, just returned from a retreat in the mountains, regretting that I've already stashed my suitcase away. I should have left it on my bedroom floor, mouth open like a baby bird waiting to be fed, anxious to leave the nest.

Leaving Home: A Journey to Ourselves

Published in 1990, many, many years after my childhood and
that of my children, Dr. Seuss's book *Oh, The Places You'll Go!*
has a revered place on my bookshelf — close at hand and often
opened. I bring it to each Wild Women writing workshop for
our Life Journeys sessions, and, after reading it aloud to the
women, showing the illustrations on each page as I imagine a
schoolteacher would, I place it on our altar.

> Congratulations!
> Today is your day.
> You're off to Great Places!
> You're off and away!

My father was born under the sign of Sagittarius, the wanderer of the zodiac. My friend Dian, who'll say an immediate
yes to almost any invitation to go on a journey, blames her wanderlust on her Sagittarian influence. And though, in astrology-
speak, I have Sagittarius rising, I blame my wayfaring ways
on my father. He's the one who sat me down on the sofa with
the invitation to "come have a look." He spread the big green
pre–World War II atlas across both our laps and took me on a
tour of the world, page by page, map by map, finally coming
to the solar system, the pictures of the planets bright against a
deep, black sky. I tell him Venus is my favorite and that one day
I want to go there. "I'll be a Venusian," I say.

"The Universe," Daddy says, tracing a finger over the inky
expanse. "Nobody can say how it came to be or how big it is
or where it begins or ends." He and I fell quiet then, on that
scratchy brown sofa, dreaming the dreams of natural-born
travelers.

If I still had that big atlas I would have placed it on the altar, too, such was its significance to me. Instead I placed my car keys there. While I traveled here and there as a young girl — Girl Scout camp, vacations with my family that usually involved a place for Daddy to fish, a car trip with my best girlfriend's family, and of course, my family's great migration halfway across the country to our new home in California — my true journeying began when I got my first car and could go it alone — anytime, anywhere.

"The literature of women's lives is a tradition of escapees, women who have lived to tell the tale," wrote Phyllis Rose in *The Norton Book of Women's Lives*. "They resist captivity. They get up and go."

EXPLORATION: You're Off and Away!

For this Exploration, write about a time you went "roving." It could be as an escapee from normal life, an early adventure into a world about which you weren't very worldly, or a tentative toe stuck in the wanderlust waters. Let wild voice rove among memories and experiences.

Journeys Taken / Journeys Remembered

To my mind, there are tourists and there are travelers. Tourists are those who go with a planned itinerary, one often planned by someone else. Rooms are reserved, expeditions are arranged, often with tickets purchased ahead of time; all the right clothes are packed and lists of what to bring back for those at home are tucked away with the return-trip tickets. I have taken these kinds of trips myself. And enjoyed them.

Travelers, though, operate from a different mind-set — the wildish way of journeying. This manner of traveling is often the result of a hunger to discover something we might not be able to name. It may be more of an instinctual urge that comes to us on the breeze, lifting the summer curtains as we sit beside the window, lost in daydreams. Or when we suddenly look up from the book we're reading and find ourselves wondering how soon we can take a few weeks off work. It's the urge, as we are doing a Google search for information on fatty acids, that finds us clicking to a map of Thailand.

"It's time," this yearning says, and you recognize the voice of your wild self, and the "something" you weren't able to identify is calling your name.

Surprisingly and wonderfully enough, this longing can happen upon us even while we're happily gallivanting along as tourists and, if we heed the call, this is when we deviate from our well-laid plans and chuck the tickets for the bus tour of Irish castles and go off on our own, driving on the opposite side of the road less traveled.

"You do not travel if you are afraid of the unknown, you travel for the unknown, that reveals you with yourself," said Ella Maillart, traveler, adventurer, and journalist and one of those Wild Women, along with Miriam Beard, Isabel Bird, Beryl Markham, and others of our forebears in whose footprints we place our own brave feet. This is what our wild nature asks of us.

In her stunning book *Wild*, writing of her decision to walk alone the 2,650 miles of the Pacific Coast Trail, Cheryl Strayed said, "I'd finally come to understand what it had been: a yearning for a way out, when actually what I had wanted to find was a way in."

EXPLORATION: Journeys Taken

This Exploration calls for you to create a scatterpage of journeys taken and/or journeys remembered. Remember, the scatter-page effect may offer a richer source for story than a thoughtful chronological list could. (Notice the *logical* in the word *chrono-logical*.) Attempting to list your journeys chronologically may have you hesitating as you try to remember whether you went on the cruise up the Inland Passage the year before or the year after you rode the Amtrak to New Orleans. Or was it the road trip to Big Sur?

Again, as we've done in previous Explorations, we'll select one from the scatterpage for an extended writing session, hold-ing the list in our Journey Notes for other sessions, other times.

Write the location and the date (as near as you can remem-ber) at the top of the page. When you write these facts, if you allow it, an image will come to you. This is where your inner writer is telling you it wants to begin. Begin here, and let your pen take you on this journey. Writing the story of the journey is like going on the journey twice, each time yielding its own revelations.

Answering the Call: Responding to the Inner Voice

The summer before my forty-eighth birthday, almost four years after my husband died, some flash of insight I can't explain led to me sell the business we owned together, sell the condominium I'd moved to after he died, sell the fancy-pants car I bought thinking that changing the outsides could change the insides (it does, but only a little). I put most of my belong-ings in storage, bought an around-the-world airline ticket, and left home. The only requirements: start in one direction and keep going, with no turning back, and return within a year.

I'd go on the trail of the goddesses I'd been studying. It would be an inward-outward journey, a quest for an identity as a woman alone in the world, and, I have to admit, an attempt to fulfill the longing I'd had since my father and I sat side by side on that scratchy brown sofa and paged through the world, country by country, continent by continent and beyond, to the solar system.

Years later, I was delighted to discover a book by Sue Monk Kidd, a writer I admire, who found herself near that same age, filled with that same yearning. In *Traveling with Pomegranates*, Kidd asked herself a series of questions: *"Is there an odyssey the female soul longs to make at the approach of fifty — one that has been blurred and lost within a culture awesomely alienated from soul? If so, what sort of journey would that be? Where would it take me?"*

"The impulse to go to Greece emerged out of those questions," she wrote. "It seized me before I got back to the minuscule apartment. *Greece*. That would be the portal. I would make a *pilgrimage* in search of an initiation."

I've heard many such stories, and though the outer destinations differ, the inner is always the same. Elyn Aviva wrote, in *Following the Milky Way*, "You hear a call that cannot be

> ### NOTES FOR NURTURING WILD VOICE
>
> - Listen to your intuition. Write from there.
> - Trust yourself. Trust your pen. Trust your ideas.
> - Listen to your body when you write and when you read back what you've written. Voice. Breath. Heartbeat. Gut. Listen for the thrill of yes!, the excitement of connection with your Truth, the depth of connection with your soul. Notice the fear. The anxiety. The surprise. The satisfaction.

denied — perhaps it began as whisper twenty years earlier, perhaps it began as an ear-splitting shout a week before. Soon or later, you feel compelled to respond."

Carol wrote: "On my thirty-ninth birthday I had a sudden impulse to answer a call to live a more authentic life. I called it my midlife reawakening. I was not one to take risks or live impulsively, but the call was so strong I found the strength and will to do it. In one week's time I left my alcoholic husband, home, garden, business and most of my possessions and moved across the country to recover my soul and begin my rebirth."

Odyssey. Pilgrimage. Initiation. Perhaps we don't utter these words, or even acknowledge them; we simply know it's time to go. And we may not recognize that the outward journey is truly a longing for an inward journey, a descent into the Self, where we can connect with our authenticity, heal, transition from one way of being into another, leave behind that which we have outgrown, and expand into a new consciousness.

"I've done these pilgrimages at various times to support my spiritual and creative lives," wrote Camille, "to reconnect with my truth by taking a journey into myself as much as into an often unfamiliar physical location."

NOTHING TO DECLARE:
MEMOIRS OF A WOMAN TRAVELING ALONE

Mary Morris

I had grown weary of life in New York and had some money from a grant, so I felt ready for a change. With a terrible feeling of isolation and a growing belief that America had become a foreign land, I headed south. I went in search of a place where the land and the people and the time in which they lived were somehow connected — where life would begin to make sense to me again.

Sometimes this call requires that we leave the familiar, like Sue Monk Kidd, like Carol, like Camille, like Mary Morris and so many other journeyers. Like me. For others, the journey isn't to a distant place but to a place deep inside.

Pamela said the journey she embarks on when she makes art "is the most restorative, healing work that I have found that allows me to understand and change my life and how I engage it."

For others, that hunger for discovery may never be quelled. "The gypsy blood my mother talked about runs deep in our family," said Madaline. "That longing for adventure is end-less....I have accepted that there are those of us who have the wanderlust and no one journey will ever fulfill our longing."

"I am intended to be a journeywoman," wrote Morris, "a wanderer of the planet, and, I suppose, of the heart."

And still others, like Sylvia, have heard the call but have yet to respond: "When I was twenty-two and teaching at a private bilingual school in Puerto Rico, one of my students brought me a picture from a magazine — Mendoza Castle in Spain. My namesake. My family is from there and Mexico. In my heart and in my gut, I know that is a journey I have to make. The longing simmers within, still calling to me. Something wild and deep awaits me there."

EXPLORATION: Odysseys and Pilgrimages

Have you gone on a quest to attain something your heart desired or to discover or achieve something? Have you been on a journey toward something or someplace, only to discover something richer and more meaningful than your original goal?

Write of a quest you made, successful or not. Or write of a pilgrimage. Write of a journey you took, an inward/outward odyssey. Take time with your writing; slow down, go deep.

Is there a journey simmering within calling to you? Have you heard the call and answered no? Discoveries come when we let go of expectations and rules in journeying — and in writing.

Writing Our Way Home: Finding the Story in the Journey

Last fall I'd just returned from a month-long sojourn on the East Coast, and I was full to bursting with images and events and characters. I had so much I wanted to write about, I found myself paralyzed by infinite choice.

Should I start with swimming with the manatees in Florida's Crystal River or walking the labyrinth at the Dalí Museum in St. Petersburg? Should I attempt to describe the Jurassic-like plant life at the ancient Sunken Gardens or the surreal mermaid show at Weeki Wachee Springs? Mermaids!

Then came the road trip with Drusilla in which we drove and told stories — imagined and remembered — from Florida to New York. What about the stories inside that story?

I wanted to write about our time in beautiful historic Savannah, where I'd never been but swear I must return to. I wanted to describe the geography of the low country, the tatters of an old plantation where massive oaks lined the drive and you couldn't help but think of Scarlett O'Hara, and a visitor's center where history had been cleaned up and rewritten, and I wonder if I do that, too, with my own history.

There's more, of course, there's always more, and so

where do you start and how do you find what matters among all the details? Writing life's journeys is so much more than simply describing where you went and who you met and what they looked like and who said what to whom. It's more than what happened when.

It's the interior journey we want to take, following the trail of our words to what matters, like journeying to visit a faraway friend for a reunion of the heart. This is why we must slow down and breathe. Why we must trust the pen and our deep-knowing, inner voice. Otherwise we are just tourists, sightseers of our own lives.

As you write your life journeys, look for discoveries, connections, and the serendipity of travel — inward and outward. Look for what is lost and what is found. Find the stories in things, the revelations in place. Allow memories to surface and find their way onto the page. Explore intuitive connections — this to that, and that, and once again. Take time for reflection so insight can emerge. Where are you ready for deeper exploration? What intrigues you? Where, as you skim along pen to page, do you go "hmmm?" Where do emotions arise? Pay attention. Listen. Be present. Remember to breathe.

So...
be your name Buxbaum or Bixby or Bray
or Mordecai Ali Van Allen O'Shea,
You're off to Great Places!
Today is your day!
Your mountain is waiting.
So...get on your way!

Continuing the Journey:
Further Explorations into Life Journeys

1. Have you ever been lost, only to discover something or someplace you never would have found had you stayed on course?

2. Sometimes in our travels we find ourselves in places or situations where we feel surprisingly comfortable and at home. Other times we may experience the vague feeling of having been in a place before, not déjà vu, exactly, but a feeling akin to it. Where and when have you experienced this kind of connection?

3. Have you ever met someone on a journey, and did the connection change your life, even though you may never have seen or heard from the person again?

4. Pico Iyer wrote, "We travel, initially, to lose ourselves; and we travel, next, to find ourselves. We travel to open our hearts and eyes and learn more about the world than our newspapers will accommodate....And we travel, in essence, to become young fools again — to slow time down and get taken in, and fall in love once more."

    When, during your journeys, have you fallen in love?

5. Ah, the serendipity of being in the right place at the right time: a spectacular sunset just as you summit a peak; a speaker or entertainer or teacher you've always wanted to meet who just happens to be in the town you never expected to visit on that particular journey; coming upon an old friend from home lounging on a park bench in the middle of a strange city or in the same train compartment from point A to point B, or...you get the idea.

    Take the writing beyond the serendipitous event itself

to its deeper meaning. Did you discover something about yourself while witnessing that sunset? Did the connection with the old friend create something new in your relationship? Go beyond the anecdote of the event to its deeper effect.

Notes from the Journey

1. Do you take your Journey Notes with you when you go on journeys? I try to make a practice of writing both morning and evening when I'm traveling. The time is often so full and, with travel, I find myself more receptive and aware, noticing so much. I want to be sure to get some of the details down before they become muddied.

2. I also find myself more susceptible to emotions when traveling — a sunset can bring me to tears; I'm easily overcome with homesickness; sometimes anxiety gets the better of me, especially when I'm lost, which happens more often than I care to admit. And when writing about journeys taken and journeys remembered, these emotions make themselves felt again; writing is a way to give them expression.

3. Have you heard the whispered call of the next journey? What does your wild self want?

11 WHERE THE WILD THINGS ARE
Illuminating the Shadow

If you want to find your brightest light then you need to look in your darkest room.

— Gina Mollicone-Long

Chiaroscuro is an art technique that uses both deep variations and subtle gradations of light and shading — shadow — for dramatic effect. Without shadow, images have no dimension, character delineation is flat — a character in a cartoon versus a figure painted by Caravaggio. So it is with us Wild Women. We are the human equivalent of chiaroscuro, an embodiment of light and shadow.

Over the years, in our Wild Women writing workshops, some participants have become a little skittish as we near the session on Shadow. Not completely undeserved, Shadow has a bad reputation. We call her our dark side, the other, our repressed self, our evil twin. But Shadow is also creative, spontaneous, original, imaginative, and very, very juicy. Within these depths, out of view, true passion dwells.

It's from Jung and his followers and practitioners that we come to our current definition and understanding of Shadow. Jung tells us that at an early age we begin to separate from and then repress whatever parts of us don't seem acceptable in the world around us. When we get those certain looks from parents or reprimands from teachers, when we're scolded or punished for behaviors or actions or attitudes, we get the message: if you want approval and to be accepted, don't do that, be that, say that, think that. It's from this early age we begin to haul Shadow around with us, an expandable bag of parts of us labeled "don't."

This isn't all bad, and much of it is necessary — we can't just go around taking what we want, especially when it belongs to others, or intentionally hurting other people, or destroying what someone else has created just because it doesn't suit our taste. Jealousy doesn't serve anyone except artists, who can transform it in their work. To get along in whatever culture we're born into, we need to follow certain mores. But among those "don'ts" that we shove into our bag are perceptions based on our little kid self, which may not hold up in our adult lives. I still don't know why I feel like I have to make my bed every day or why I feel guilty about the hours I keep, or that two of my four basic food groups are prepared in the microwave, and one of them is popcorn.

Shadow and the Creative Life

The truth is, for us to be whole and to live authentically and to be able to write from our authentic wildness, we must shine a light into the darkness and claim all of ourselves. We may think what we'll discover will be unbearable, but it won't be. Ask any practitioner of shadow work; Shadow contains positive aspects as well as negative, and what at first appears negative can have its positive effects. In *The Shadow Effect*, Debbie Ford wrote, "Far from frightening, embracing the shadow allows us to be whole, to be real, to take back our power, to unleash our passions, and to realize our dreams."

It isn't just in childhood that we put away those shadowy

aspects of ourselves; we do it in our creative lives, too. If we're discouraged or censored in our creative expression, we may begin to censor ourselves so that what shows up on the page is either a lie or a tame rendition of what we really want to say. We may even stop writing (or painting or composing) all together. I've seen this happen all too often. Students come to class scared, and admit they haven't written since (fill in the hurtful blank), but then here they are, willing to risk again. That urge to write just won't go away. "Good for you," I say, "welcome back." I'm sorry for the ones who never get back, and sad for what unique expression doesn't get added to the world, but I understand. It took me decades after a shunning experience in high school before I dared make any kind of messy art again, and I'm still an embarrassingly shy artist, barely braving a book art class or mosaic workshop, even when the instructor is a close friend.

It's true, too, that there's a fine line between creativity and madness, and we have plenty of examples of the line being crossed: Van Gogh's genius and delusions, Nijinsky, who finally was unable to perform, Virginia Woolf and Sylvia Plath and Anne Sexton and too many others who took their own lives. Writers and poets seem to be especially afflicted.

Fearing, perhaps, that we may have a touch of madness or might be judged as weird, we refuse our quirks and eccentricities, relegating them to Shadow, when it may be those very quirks that are the hallmark of our original wild voice.

FOR EACH OF YOU

Audre Lorde

Be who you are and will be
learn to cherish

that boisterous Black Angel that drives you
up one day and down another
protecting the place where your power rises
running like hot blood
from the same source
as your pain.

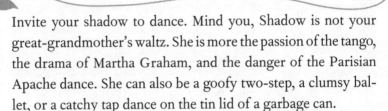

EXPLORATION: Dance with Your Shadow

Invite your shadow to dance. Mind you, Shadow is not your great-grandmother's waltz. She is more the passion of the tango, the drama of Martha Graham, and the danger of the Parisian Apache dance. She can also be a goofy two-step, a clumsy ballet, or a catchy tap dance on the tin lid of a garbage can.

Dance with Shadow, and she will want to lead. Let her. It may be a delicious freedom to dance with such wild abandon. Remember the Allen Ginsberg Mind Writing Slogan: "Follow your inner moonlight; don't hide your madness."

In this Exploration, start with the prompt "I would never, but Shadow would…" and surrender your pen to Shadow's lead. Here it's more important than ever not to think! Thinking is exactly what your ego would have you do. Ego's job, after all, is to protect and defend you against those shadowy impulses and actions. But this is how wild voice gets stifled.

One way to write this Exploration is through a list poem. A list poem is an ancient form found in the Bible (all those begats), the *Illiad* (Homer's list of heroes) and one of my favorites, Sei Shōnagon's *Pillow Book* (Rare Things, Moving Things, Things that Should Not Be Seen by Firelight).

A list poem is an inventory. Follow the prompt with a list of things you would never say or do or write or even think but

Shadow would. The list poem doesn't have to rhyme, but it can. Write the list as it comes to you. You can rearrange and shape it later. Be sure to read it aloud; rhythm is key to a good list poem. Remember, no thinking, and no censoring. (Shadow doesn't censor, one of the things that got her in trouble in the first place.)

You may find, among those items in your list, something that's been shoved away in Shadow's bag that doesn't belong there anymore (if it ever did). You may find some intrigues, some temptations that could be treats. You may also find some things that need forgiving or nurturing or that need to be brought up into the light, where they can thrive.

Accepting Shadow, Using Her Gifts

All those real emotions we experience — the anger, the jealousy, the desire, the wounding grief, the black moods, our deep pain — feelings we're told to "just get over," or the ones we sense make others uncomfortable — all these can be found among the detritus that's been stuffed in Shadow's pockets. Yet these are the very emotions that we writers can make great use of.

You can write about a mother's loss of her son or daughter to war, but if you use abstract words for emotion rather than showing the emotion itself, the mother won't really feel the depth of her pain, nor will the reader, nor will you. We can't keep ourselves distant and removed if we're to write from our deep wildness. You may not be a mother who has lost a child, but you are human and that means you cannot escape sorrow; the world is drowning in sorrow.

To write into the depths, give your sorrow to the page, open your heart and let it speak its hunger, unleash the jealousy that roils your guts and tempts you to ram your car into "that woman's" house, let it run rampant through your fingers and onto the blank screen of your monitor where it can pant, uncensored and unjudged. Use it; use it all. This is how art can save us.

Many keep journals where they write these dark emotions, writing through to the other side. I hope you are using your Journey Notes as a receptacle for what can't be expressed another way. My morning journal is filled with longings that would make me sound pitiful to my friends and bore anyone but my therapist, though I expect therapists are pretty good at masking their yawns. I also record the pettiness and the jealousies and the righteous anger. *Ay yi yi.* These exposures of my darker side are among the reasons I think of destroying my journals. But here's the thing: days or weeks later, when I read back what I've written about someone else, I often see that what's caused me to react in a way that I have to write out to get through is something I recognize in myself — a behavior, a habit, a careless slight. Oh, I say. And there's the light.

> ### NOTES FOR NURTURING WILD VOICE
>
> - Be as messy as you need to be.
> - Tell the truth.
> - Risk embarrassing yourself.
> - Feel the anxiety. Stay in the chair. Stay in the room.

This is one of the gifts that comes when we open the door and shout into the darkness, "Who's there?" "It's me," is the answer in a reenactment of that famous quote from the Pogo comic strip, "We have met the enemy and he is us."

What I see in you, I see in myself. We are all the same; it's only a matter of degrees. This is where compassion is born, out of Shadow by way of light. It's this compassion that will enable us to write our deepest truth without righteous judgment and to write wild with our authentic voice.

EXPLORATION: Me and My Shadow

Drusilla named the risk-taking, defensive aspect of her character Nadia. "Nadia has gotten me in trouble plenty of times," she writes. "Her motto has always been carpe diem. She smoked and drank and did drugs and stayed up writing half the night. She encourages the part of me that says *fuck you*, and at the same time I can trace the way she has encouraged me to take chances throughout my life, urged me on when I was afraid, stood up for me, too."

Does your shadow have a name? Does she speak to you? If so, what does she say? What does she wear? Who does she look like? Do you love her in spite of it all? I posed these questions in a blog post. Following is a response I received from Linda.

My shadow, she who has no name, as she has no need for that, has a picture of herself, which she pasted into my album. Changing her face to look like me, she wears chocolate on her nose as, with an ecstatic look on her face, she licks out a huge cereal bowl of gone ice cream. The Unnamed was overjoyed to find she had done something indecorous and sent me to the store for more, while with rock blaring from the old-fashioned ghetto blaster she mad-danced in my living room. She sleeps beside me, too, sometimes and wakes me to say look who's here, and sometimes she just hovers in a corner and watches the predawn street. Other times when I awaken in the coddled darkness she whispers that I should get up and keep her company while she plots and schemes. Her clothes are long and flow with the nuances of a silky breeze or breath as she prances where she will. I love her madly. She teaches me many things.

Now it's your turn. Close your eyes and let images of your shadow appear. Does music accompany her appearance? What is the sound of her voice, the color of her eyes? What does Shadow want to tell you?

Giving Voice to Shadow's Roar

Wild Women are not docile, and wild voice doesn't always sing sotto voce. Anger wants to speak; rage must be expressed. To be authentic is also to feel what has been called "women's rage." This may be the darkest shadow side, the most unwelcome place, exactly what mother told us not to feel. But here it is, and if we are to live an authentic life, its release is mandatory, not in a white-hot fire that scorches all life to cinders, but with flames contained, as in the necessary wilderness fires that protect ecosystems and make way for new growth.

What good can come of anger? I think of Elizabeth Cady Stanton, Susan B. Anthony, Lucretia Mott, and other suffragettes. I think of Rosa Parks refusing to give up her seat on the bus and Candy Lightner, who turned her grief and rage into Mothers Against Drunk Driving, its acronym especially appropriate: MADD.

Rage contained, expressed, and learned from can become art.

The novels of Toni Morrison, the poetry of Adrienne Rich. Eve Ensler's play *The Vagina Monologues*, which began off Broadway in 1996 and evolved into V-Day, a worldwide movement that raises millions of dollars for women's anti-violence groups. These and thousands of other works illustrate how Shadow's roar can be transformed by writers and artists into expressions of truth and beauty.

EXPLORATION: Out of Shadow, Art

Themes of rage and anger have appeared many times in the stories and poems and personal narratives that are written and read in my workshops; I've written more than a few of my own, giving a gun to this character and a knife to that one. One particular story of revenge I wrote in a writing practice session gave me a little scare as I wrote it and a bigger one when I read it aloud the first time.

Am I really capable of killing someone, then using his scalp as a cloth on an altar to the god of lies? Holy moley! Where does this stuff come from?

In many ways, our writing, like our dreams, allows us to act out in ways we never would in real life. Ego and rational thought aren't allowed in dreamworld and shouldn't be invited into our just-get-it-down writing, either.

Let the Dark Angel of your anger or rage find its voice through a poem or a story. Write a memory that still stirs the blood. Maybe you'll hear another voice that questions whether you're sure you want to write it — the censor or the editor. But, maybe, as other courageous writers have done, you'll continue anyway.

I've mentioned that I take more risks and often write more authentically when I'm working in the company of other writers, especially writers I trust. Maybe you'll want to get together with one or two other Wild Women writers for some timed writing Explorations, leaving room at the table for your Dark Angels to contribute if they want.

Remember, no one has to see what you've written. You're free to tear it up or burn it and stuff the ashes down the garbage disposal. But maybe you won't want to. Maybe you'll see how that raw, uncensored piece can be transformed into something remarkable and real.

Turn anger into satire, as Margaret Atwood does. Use dark humor in the manner of Dorothy Parker. Let rage be acted out by fictional characters.

This is where timed writing can help. Set your timer for fifteen or seventeen minutes; begin writing, and don't stop until the time's up. Really. Don't go back and read what you've written until the time's up. Don't edit, scratch out, or revise until the time's up, and even then, don't be in a hurry to censor the work. Let all that white-hot energy have its voice.

The Gift of Shadow

Deep voice is more like a rich chord than a single note. Our characters would be dull without their shadow, as would we, as writers and women. Shadow lends depth, and from depth comes authenticity.

Shadow is both teacher and resource. A place where the heart of creative energy and originality beats, wild and steady. When we shine the light of acceptance onto what we previously turned away from and integrate it into our lives as best we can, we become stronger and wiser and more complete. We belong to ourselves again, and from this place we do our work.

Continuing the Journey:
Further Explorations into Where the Wild Things Are

1. Has your shadow brought you experiences that you otherwise wouldn't have had? Write them, and write how they affected you, changed you, told you something about yourself you didn't know.

2. Write a monologue in the voice of your Dark Angel. What does she want? What's her side of the story?

3. If one of our shadow aspects causes us to be a perfectionist, we can never be free to write from our wild voice. Wild implies uncontrolled, and the uncontrolled, free-fall of writing from that deepest, most authentic place can be frightening, even if we're not perfectionists.

   Does perfectionism keep you from letting 'er rip in your writing, even in the first raw mess of a draft? Explore the voice of the perfectionist. What does she say? Where did it come from?

   While you're at it, take a look at the voice of the censor. The censor may think it's protecting you, but what it's really doing is blocking access to free expression of your wildish nature. What has the censor kept you from writing?

4. In some of the more creative writing practice sessions I've experienced, I've turned my pen over to a persona and let her write the story. Loretta is a woman of varied and colorful sexual appetites and is especially given to cowboys. Jolene can't help but fall for the wrong man, which gets her into situations that she doesn't always get out of by the end of the writing time. We all like Aunt Boochie, who drinks and smokes and has a wicked sense of humor; Aunt Boochie never lies. Then there's "you," that second-person character who is never identified but who

tells some truths and takes some chances and dares morality but who is never "I." "You" is the persona who has deepest access to shadowland and who has given me what I consider some of my most authentic work.

Explore your deep voice via a persona. You don't have to know anything about this character when you set out. Characteristics and voice will evolve as you surrender to what he or she has to say. Any prompt will work with persona; just respond to the prompt with the persona's voice instead of writing in the first-person as yourself.

5. As we do the work of claiming our wildness and giving it voice, we may be surprised by the anger — sometimes rage — that comes to the surface.

"Anger is meant to be listened to," counsels Julia Cameron. But often we don't listen to our anger; we "stuff it, deny it, bury it, block it, hide it, lie about it, medicate it, muffle it, ignore it." This is where writing can serve you. Let the page receive your anger. Write until the paper tears, until the lead breaks, until the pen leaves splotches of ink, like blood, on the page. Write and write and write and write through your anger to the other side. You may discover there's something to be done — not in anger, but in the calm aftermath of the storm, where the cleanup work begins.

6. Times of deep emotions can also be times when creativity swells with urgency. It's as if the barrier that has held back pain or sorrow or anger has been broken through, and we descend into that dark well where emotion merges with creativity and out of the depths rises poetry or song or dance or images pulsing with feeling. The deepest song is filled with the truest emotion.

But sometimes ego doesn't want us to descend. After my father died I was afraid to write about his death, afraid any words I wrote would take me to the edge of a black hole that I would fall into and never come out. Fear kept me paralyzed, my pen still. But I now know that Shadow would have welcomed me, would have offered me what I needed to give expression to my grief.

I hope when you experience difficult times, you'll have the courage to descend into the well and let Shadow's creativity buoy you and carry you through the storm.

Notes from the Journey

1. As we passed through shadowy territory, did your handwriting change as you wrote your daily Journey Notes? Sometimes when I'm writing what feels dangerous, my handwriting gets smaller; letters get more cramped and are often transposed. Frequent misspellings show up, too, like rocks along the path. I also find I cross out more often, or fall into several false starts before I can get into the rhythm of the writing. Just don't quit, I tell myself. Don't quit.

2. Falling under Shadow's creative spell, it's easy to lose track of time. When I'm in the groove, the last thing I want to do is stop to prepare a meal, or even eat. Everything I know tells me that we produce more and better if we take breaks and get up and take a walk, even if it's just three times around the room. But Shadow seems to like binge creativity. Balance, I tell her, we need balance. Can you keep your balance during creative binges?

3. I almost always light a candle when I write, but I find the ritual of lighting it and placing it on my writing table, and the constancy of the flame, especially meaningful when I do shadow work. Have you noticed that *ritual* is contained in the word *spiritual*?

12 DREAMS AND SYNCHRONICITY
The Intuitive Wisdom
of Wild Women

You have to leave the city of your comfort and go into the wilderness of your intuition. What you'll discover will be wonderful. What you'll discover is yourself.

— Alan Alda

Women know the transformative powers of a hot bath. Maybe it's the weightless relief of being up to your neck in warm water, or the hypnotic flickering of candlelight, the way a misty room can absorb audible sighs. Magic can happen under such circumstances.

It was chilly that November night, and the little studio above a garage I'd taken as a writing space felt especially cold. To warm my bones, I lit the candles, drew a steamy bath, fragranced up the bathroom, and climbed into the tub. The writing wasn't going that well, anyhow. In fact, my life in general was in a bit of a stuck place between this and that, without my having even an idea of the next thing, being just past one of those birthdays that gives you pause. I leaned back, eyes closed, soaking, when suddenly I was struck with an idea so clear, so fully formed, so powerful that its very energy knocked a candle from the edge of the tub and into the steaming water.

A writing center! I would open a writing center.

The idea came complete, as if it descended whole through the clouds of steam. I would create a place where writers could come together; we'd form a community of support for writers of all stripes — even those who didn't know they were writers yet. We'd have classes and workshops and readings and literary salons, maybe a bookstore.

I scrambled out of the tub, wrapped myself in my robe and my hair in a towel, and stumbled, dripping, into the other room, where I grabbed my journal and began making notes. Pages and pages of notes. The concept, the bones of a business plan, even rough sketches of the furniture arrangement in the salon.

"One of the most remarkable things about using intuition and the instinctive nature is that is causes a surefooted spontaneity to erupt," writes Dr. Estés. My experience that November night nearly twenty-five years ago was surely an eruption, like Vesuvius itself, and its power forever altered my world.

Intuition: Knowing Without Reasoning

Whole libraries of books have been written about intuition. Scientific studies, philosophical and theosophical treatises, books and essays and papers by experts and wonderers alike. Neurologists try to pin it down to a function of the brain, a specific region — all those limbic and primitive parts. Those of a more holistic or spiritual bent attribute it to something more mysterious, connected not only to an inner knowing but also to a universal creative force that links us all. Some scientists and great thinkers live in both worlds and not only acknowledge the existence of this sixth sense that defies logical explanation but embrace it. Albert Einstein called the intuitive mind a sacred gift, and Jonas Salk said, "It is always with excitement that I wake up in the morning wondering what my intuition will toss up to me, like gifts from the sea. I work with it and rely on it. It's my partner."

Getting back to the Writing Center for a moment.

There's that great line from *Field of Dreams:* "If you build it, they will come." Well, I did and they did. The original organization had a brief but memorable five-year life span. Some years later a second nonprofit literary organization, San Diego Writers, Ink, formed, phoenix-like, from its ashes and is thriving today.

But this is not the end of the story; there's more.

Long after the original writing center closed, I recalled something I'd been told by a psychic several years before that life-altering vision in my bathtub. As we sat together in her boho apartment in San Francisco, Carol revealed that not only were the boyfriend from whom I was then estranged and I going to be together again, but we were going to build a creative center. "Not exactly a school," she said, "but a center where people would come together to write and make art."

Intuition? Synchronicity? Messages from whatever gods or benevolent spirits might exist? This is where it gets all murky and where my logical mind gets boggled and where trying to figure it all out is best abandoned to the mysterious depths that exist outside the bounds of logic.

Intuition: The "Treasure of a Woman's Psyche"

As it was with Einstein and Salk, so it is with writers and artists, musicians and dancers, all creative beings. This gift that comes to us from the sea or the sky or the mysterious beyond or from our own depths is a treasure of the wild soul that we can trust for guidance in our work and in our lives. It is our most valuable asset and the way to our deepest truth.

Shakti Gawain, who has written extensively about intuition, said, "One of the sure ways to know if you're following your intuition is that you feel more alive. You may feel a little scared, or anxious, or excited…but one thing for sure is that there's an aliveness to it."

This is what I find with writers who begin to trust their intuitive voice — this scared aliveness that accompanies the first tentative forays. Writing from this place can cause your hand to shake and your heart to skitter. You may forget to breathe. When we write from this place we're no longer playing it safe; we may be breaking some rules, telling some secrets, but by damn! we're writing from our most authentic wildness. Once we learn to listen with deep hearing, an open mind, and willing hands, other surprising things may happen. Our language becomes more expansive and inventive, and the rhythm of the words catches the rhythm of our breath, our heartbeat. We write things we didn't know we knew. "Where did that come from?" we ask.

EXPLORATION: First Sighting

When I asked women about their first recognition that they were intuitive beings, or what their first intuitive experience was, many said they couldn't recall the time or the incident. "It was with me long before I had a name for it," Jill said.

Recognition comes upon us like dawn — light exists before we see the actual sun. How do you know what you know? Can you trust it? Do you talk about it? Do you encourage it? Do you fight against it or bless it?

This is Anitra's story of an intuitive experience.

Around 8:30 on a Saturday morning, I got a feeling that something bad was happening to Holly. I knew clearly that it wasn't anyone else and I could feel that there was danger. But I still resisted the idea of extrasensory knowledge. I did not want people to categorize me with woo-woo new age weirdos talking to spirits and channeling Queen Victoria. I dismissed my strange fears for Holly as random thoughts.

But the feeling of dread about her continued for the rest of Saturday. And all day Sunday. Finally, on Sunday evening I called.

"Holly, you're going to think this is ridiculous, but all weekend I've had this feeling that something bad is going on with you. I know it sounds really dumb."

"What time did the feeling start, Anita?"

"Right around 8:30 yesterday morning."

"That was exactly the time I arrived at the ER with my dad, who was having a heart attack. I've been in the ER and then the ICU with him all weekend."

Afterward, I couldn't ignore the fact that a second experience couldn't be so easily dismissed as chance. I tossed my hubris out the window and admitted that there are powerful and valid experiences that we don't understand.

Intuition, this deep-seeing, deep-hearing messenger from our wild nature, is always with us, though we may not always know to listen to it or how to interpret its messages. Many books and websites offer exercises for enhancing or developing your intuition. Most often these begin with "quiet the mind" or "be still." So it is with writing from your authentic wildness. Quiet the mind, be still and be present, and allow the words and images to come through you.

Close your eyes and remember a time you "knew without reasoning." Recall the feeling and how you responded.

Write about your experience with your clear light of inner knowing. Tell the story of your first sighting or an intuitive experience that had a profound effect on you. Look for the layers of understanding.

Synchronicity: A Jungian Term for a Wild Phenomenon

Serendipity. Kismet. Divine providence. Lovely, magical words that are often used to talk about synchronicity. *Coincidence,* a less lovely, less magical term, is the one most often used to describe this remarkable phenomenon, along with *being in the right place at the right time, sheer luck, lucky break, happy chance, happenstance, circumstance.*

Some say synchronicity is the same thing as intuition, or nearly the same. One is an outer manifestation, the other an inner knowing. The two may be close cousins of clairvoyance and precognition. You're thinking of someone, and voilà! they call you on the phone; you're considering buying a new car but can't decide between ragtop or moonroof, and in the next half-hour see a dozen moonroofed cars; three participants in a writing workshop, unbeknownst to one another, use the same unusual phrase or image that isn't directly related to the prompt they're given.

Explaining Jung's concept of the term he coined can get deep into the weeds of psychological theory pretty quickly.

Those of us who would rather have the experience than the explanation may prefer to allow the mystery of it to give us shivers and, perhaps, hope that there is indeed some underlying order to the Universe. Life is not random; we are connected to one another and to something larger.

When I wrote to some Wild Women friends and colleagues, writers and nonwriters alike, many responded with stories of synchronicity.

Anitra said: "I wanted to know about the breeze in San Diego for an article: on a plane, I found myself sitting next to a California climatologist who gave me a succinct explanation of what I wanted to know."

Earlier I related the story of my pilgrimage to the place in the country where I lived with my husband and where his ashes were scattered, and the magical visitation by the hummingbird. Other women mentioned birds in their comments about synchronicity. Carol wrote about the hawk, which she describes as the messenger bird that comes to you when you're about to discover your life purpose. "I didn't believe in animal totems until hawks began to appear in all the places I'd always frequented," she said. "They flew out of trees, circled above in the sky, cried to me from the obscurity of the clouds, and even came to me in my dreams."

It was a while after the hawks began to appear that Carol returned to writing, which she'd loved as a child but had

> ### NOTES FOR NURTURING WILD VOICE
>
> - Banish shame.
> - Write from your passion. If you don't care about what you're writing, neither will your readers (if you have them or want them).
> - Congratulate yourself when you've written something in your authentic voice (you'll know when you've done it).

abandoned in later life. When she began her novel, the hawks disappeared, but each time she needed a reminder they would reappear.

The mystery of synchronicity isn't just that certain things occur coincidentally — I buy a particular loaf of bread and the shopper right next to me buys the same loaf of bread, which is mere coincidence — but that what occurs is meaningful. Jung theorizes that synchronicities occur when a strong need arises in the psyche of an individual. This is why the book you need tumbles out of the bookshelf into your hands, or the friend you're thinking of whom you haven't seen in years suddenly calls or writes or, even more dramatically, appears in person. Then there are the deeper, more psychological occurrences that may involve dreams or visions, events that come awfully close to what might be labeled precognition, like the following experience Judy, a participant in a Wild Women writing workshop, wrote about.

"What is it like to die?"

I turned and saw [my grandson] urgently clutching his throat.

"I mean, Grandma...is it like you want to breathe and can't?"

I was sure he was talking about my mom — his granny — who had palliatively slipped beyond a drug-induced stupor into the Mystical Hereafter. I spoke of feeling sad and my relief that she no longer suffered, then we did a review of obvious things people don't need after death, including breath. Our exchange was heartwarming, but unremarkable until the following day.

Behind closed doors in her home across the street, my neighbor lady's body was discovered. We may never know exactly when or why she chose to hang herself to death.

EXPLORATION: The Synchronicity of Synchronicity

Sometimes synchronicities can seem convenient, even efficient, responses from a benevolent Universe or other mysterious source, such as in the case of Anitra's need for information about the summer breeze and the synchronistic seating arrangement on the airplane. Other times they're like a sly wink from that same mysterious source — the occasions of writers using the identical image or words — that seem to confirm there's "magic afoot."

For this Exploration, write about your experiences with different levels of synchronicities. Rather than just writing the facts of what happened, allow your imagination to freely roam the incidents. Follow the path of words and images to what might reveal itself from your deepest intuition.

Dreams: Gifts of the Night

Like our heartbeat and our breath, our intuition continues its work even while we sleep, speaking to us in the language of the night: dreams.

In our dreams people appear in the least likely of places, and strangers bring us mysterious messages. Shape-shifting and time travel and all manner of images and symbols appear and disappear, then appear again. Dreams can answer questions and solve problems. They can influence our writing and, in turn, our creative work can alter our dreams.

Myths from various cultures tell of gods and goddesses

who spoke to certain people through dreams; others hold that the soul, or some part of it, moved out of the body and visited the places and persons the dreamer sees in her sleep. Ancient Egyptians believed that dreams were like oracles, and they would travel to a sanctuary or shrine to lie down on special "dream beds" in the hopes of receiving comfort or healing from the gods.

Enticing good dreams, staving off bad dreams, ingesting a particular food or drink that is reputed to cause a certain quality of dream — in these ways we attempt to influence the nocturnal work of the intuition. But our inner knowing has its own agenda, and dreams are yet another messenger sent to reveal our most soulful longing and our deepest understanding.

Like the language of myths and folktales, the language of dreams is symbolic and revealed through metaphor and imagery. What appears on the surface of a dream is often a watery reflection of something more meaningful that swims below.

My friend Barbara says that when she works with dream symbology, her dreams tell her a great deal about what is going on with her on an unconscious level, and sometimes they provide food for art making.

Angie also interprets the symbology of her dreams: "Recently I had a dream about breasts and the color blue," she wrote. "The Universe telling me that I am still injured in my heart and that play is necessary to heal."

Sylvia reported that her current novel came to her when she was awakened in the wee hours of the morning by a far-off train whistle, which lured to her think, "What if...," those two most magical words to fiction writers. "My protagonist, awakened by the lonely whistle of a train, follows it and leaves

everything behind to find it, jumping on and starting on a journey with strangers. She trusts she must make this trip."

Sylvia began her novel but then continued to wonder if the
dream might have a deeper meaning. "Perhaps this vision is
mirroring a desire for my own journey to an unknown place, a
place I need to find, a place where answers to unspoken questions will unfold." When I read this from Sylvia I recalled what
she'd written about the castle in Spain that's named for her
family and the journey she has yet to take.

"The dream world is the territory of the writer or artist,"
said Deena Metzger. "It may happen that the writer is the citi-
zen of no other country, but the dream world is his native land
and his citizenship cannot be revoked."

SONG OF A DREAM

Sarojini Naidu

Once in the dream of a night I stood
Lone in the light of a magical wood,
Soul-deep in visions that poppy-like sprang;
And spirits of Truth were the birds that sang,
And spirits of Love were the stars that glowed,
And spirits of Peace were the streams that flowed
In that magical wood in the land of sleep.

Keeping a dream journal not only gives us information
about our deeper selves, but it also helps us develop our intuition. If we take the time to listen to them and interpret their language, dreams can provide answers to many questions whose
solution isn't always obvious to our rational, waking mind.

Research tells us we forget half our dream within the first
five minutes of waking, and after ten minutes, 90 percent of it

is gone. This is why those who suggest keeping dream journals recommend we keep our pens and notebooks beside our beds and write our dreams immediately upon waking.

But even if we don't keep an actual dream journal, we can use the image-drenched stories brought to us by dreams in our writing or art.

EXPLORATION: Messages from the Night

In *The Finishing School*, Gail Goodwin's character Justin said, "Dreams say what they mean, but they don't say it in daytime language." So the language in which we write our dreams may be surrealistic, may be coded with symbols and images; who knows what may come when we communicate with the messengers of the night. Here is a dream I recorded during a workshop:

DREAM ORANGES

Gifts of the Night Writing Retreat (2012)

The stranger who came in her dream wore a leather hat and carried a bag of oranges. He offered her one and said he'd just picked them that day.

They could be magical, he said. He was wearing a long leather cowboy coat lined with cloth that gleamed when the sun struck it, its folds and creases like waves in a slow-moving river.

I believe in magic, she said and took the orange from his hand.   .

Careful of the seeds, he said, and from his bag he withdrew a small pouch. Put them here. They're going to feed the poor.

Do they eat the seeds? she asked. Her mother had always told her to spit the seeds out.

Watch, he said, and swallowed a handful of seeds. From his hands grew the tiniest seedlings, one on each finger, and they grew as she watched, like a Disney movie, magic and animated, until they were too large for his hands.

He dug the earth with the toe of his boot and into the hole he placed one of the seedlings and then another hole and another tree until they were surrounded by a fragrant grove.

I had not considered the deeper meaning of this dream until I retyped it for this book. As I copied it, I couldn't help but think of my husband's ashes that I spread beneath the orchard at our old property in the country. Tom has often appeared to me in dreams, riding a large dark horse and wearing a leather coat.

As so often happens when we continue to work with our intuition, whether through writing down our dreams or any of the other broad avenues into the psyche, the writing can continue to take us deeper and deeper into meaning and into that place of authentic wildness.

Write a dream you remember, even if you can recollect only a few details or images. As you write, fill in more details as they come to you, even though they may not have been in the actual dream, or you may not remember that they were. Trust your intuition — it speaks the language of dreams, which your rational mind may not know.

After you've finished writing the dream, set it aside and be still for a few moments; then return to the writing to see if more information or inner knowing has come to you about the dream. Sometimes, when you let the writing cool for days or even longer, you are rewarded with surprising insight when you return to the desk.

Continuing the Journey:
Further Explorations into Dreams and Synchronicity

1. In our first Exploration, you wrote about your "first sight-ing" of intuition, when you first knew you were an intuitive being. This Exploration asks you to continue naming and writing. The more you remember and delve into — as in a spelunking expedition — the more hidden passages and deep caverns you'll discover. Using your pen as flashlight, allow each story to reveal more evidence of your inner wisdom.

2. To receive guidance from the intuitive mind, the question to ask is not "What do I need?" but "What do I want?" Begin there.

3. In your Journey Notes, write your experiences with syn-chronicities. Make the invisible visible so you will remem-ber, and to delight and amaze yourself. Do this every day for a week, even longer. Doing this, you'll become more aware of this phenomenon; the more aware you are, the more frequently you'll experience it.

4. There are those who believe you can ask for a dream. Maybe you want the solution to a problem, or you're at a stuck place in a story, or you need an image for a poem. Before you go to sleep ask the dream maker for a dream. Keep your notebook bedside so you can record the message or any other communication that may appear.

5. Write of your premonitions, prophetic dreams, hunches that have proven true. Write of extrasensory perceptions

and communications from the other side. Make lists of these instances, select one, and do an extended writing.

6.   Who can say what or who will be our guides in life? Some Wild Women I spoke with identified animal totems — hawks and yellow birds. Sometimes we meet a stranger on a train or plane or along a trail we're following who gives us an answer to a question we might not have known we were asking. Who or what has appeared as your guide to lead you on a journey or to comfort you?

Notes from the Journey

1.   Pay attention to incidents and occurrences of intuition, and write them in a special section of your Journey Notes. Or identify an event or situation you'd like more insight about, and write it down.

2.   Too often it seems that our rational, orderly mind tells us to accomplish something, check something off our to-do list, to be productive. On the other hand, our wild nature may be telling us to go and play, or to be lazy, to sit under a leafy tree and daydream. Follow the direction of your inner guide; it knows what you need.

3.   Since the beginning of time, human beings have consulted the oracles for wisdom beyond their own understanding — the Tarot, the I-Ching, runes, and other such mediums. These oracles don't predict the future; rather, they are mirrors, directing our attention inward to where our deepest truths live. Have you considered consulting an oracle for insight into your inner knowing?

13 DEATH, LOSS, AND LEGACIES
Wise Woman

In sorrow we must go, but not in despair.
Behold! we are not bound for ever to the circles of the world,
and beyond them is more than memory.

— J. R. R. Tolkien

"We lost your grandmother," the voice on the phone said. You want to imagine everyone at a huge family picnic or maybe Disneyland, with Grandma wandering off and, well, we lost her. But that's not what the caller means. What the caller means is that Grandma is dead.

Often when we speak of death, we speak in euphemisms. One has "passed away" or "found peace" or "departed this life." A pet has "gone to a better place." We make light: "that big roundup in the sky." Or we go noir: "wearing a pine overcoat." We've got a million of them: bought the farm, bit the dust, cashed in his chips, gave up the ghost, kicked the bucket. We make religious references, too: gone on to meet his maker, gone to glory, called to God. *Dead* is a hard word to say. Hard and final.

Up until the early twentieth century, it was the family that cared for the dying, usually at home, and when death occurred, the family prepared the body for burial and sometimes even built the coffin and dug the grave. But all this has become the realm of medical professionals and caretakers in care facilities and undertakers in funeral homes. As a result, we've become distanced from death. We've become observers more than participants. With the physical distance has come a psychological distancing until, like the caller on the phone, we hesitate to utter the word *dead*.

But death is a natural part of the birth/life/death cycle, and while we humans celebrate birth and live life, when it comes to death, we approach timorously. Still, there comes a time in the work of Wild Woman for approaching the mysteries and to speak of death. That time is now.

In myths and folktales, indeed in all stories and all nature, something must die in order for something else to be born. When we look back, we can trace the life/death/life course of so many aspects of our lives: the loss of childhood as we became adults, a crisis or turning point that felt like a death but that opened the door into a new life. In our Wild Women writing workshops we acknowledge the end of our weekly meetings but begin the individual work of revising the writing that will make up the chapbook collection of our stories, which in turn, will remain as the legacy of our time together.

But what, we ask, can be the life that comes when the real and physical death of a dear one seems so final? Each of us will find our way and our meaning if, instead of putting our loss away as we're often told to do, we express it.

MACBETH, ACT 4, SCENE 3

William Shakespeare

Give sorrow words.
The grief that does not speak
whispers the o'erfraught heart
and bids it break.

For those of us for whom writing or making art is a way of expressing our response to life's experiences, out of our loss, we create. In writing from our wild depths, we bring something alive into being.

RETROSPECT IN THE KITCHEN

Maxine Kumin

After the funeral I pick
forty pounds of plums from your tree
Earth Wizard, Limb Lopper
And carry them by DC 10
Three thousand miles to my kitchen

and stand at midnight — nine o'clock
your time — on the fourth day of your death
putting some raveled things
unsaid between us into the boiling pot
of cloves, cinnamon, sugar.

Love's royal color
the burst purple fruit bob up.

EXPLORATION: Life/Death/Life

On my altar as I write this is a copy of something I wrote as my sister lay dying in a distant state. We three remaining sisters had just returned from a road trip we'd taken to see her and say our good-byes. I read the same piece at the memorial service for her a few weeks later. It begins like this:

This morning my sister's breaths came at eight per minute. This is morphine-induced sleep. This is sleep that breathes death as it approaches. The weight of it, in her air-cooled room in Clovis, New Mexico.

All morning I have been conscious of my breath. Breathing my sister in and out with my yoga practice, prayering my hands across my chest, bowing — *Namaste* — peace to you, my sister.

All morning, living in memories.

How she mimicked a singer while we played "Your Hit Parade" in our parents' bedroom, singing some sentimental song to pictures of Daddy in his navy uniform, Mama when she was in love with him, touching the lace edge of the bureau scarf...

I'll be seeing you, in all the old familiar places...

Three girls, sometimes dressed in matching dresses, in the backseat of Daddy's Nash, driving to Grandma's for Sunday dinner, driving through the Christmas-lighted park, snow-blue hills, the long echo of Daddy's horn in the tunnel, singing. Hot summer drives to a lake or a river where Daddy fished and we sat on the bank and ate cold fried chicken and bread and butter. Those days of being happy with an ice cream dipped in chocolate, those days of roller skates and bicycles and cousins and then, suddenly, my sister changed. She seemed to know things I didn't know. Mysterious things about our bodies. Secret things.

In the years since my husband died, I've written many stories, poems, and personal narrative essays not just about his death but about our time together. Memories, some of them, and fiction based on actual events, poems that attempt to capture feeling.

I've also written of my grandmothers, my mother and father, a favorite aunt who has become a recurring character in many of my flash pieces — all new life that has sprung from their lives and their deaths. This work is a way of giving voice to my sorrow and finding language for my love and loss.

This Exploration asks you to write a memory or a poem or a story of someone whose death affected you in a profound way. To bring life into the life/death/life cycle.

Considering Death

In our Wild Women writing workshops, we write to a prompt I first came across in Natalie Goldberg's book *Writing Down the Bones*. The prompt is from "Black Stone on Top of a White Stone," a poem by César Vallejo that begins:

> I shall die in Paris, in a rainstorm,
> On a day I already remember.
> I shall die in Paris — it does not bother me —
> Doubtless on a Thursday, like today, in autumn.

In our workshop we begin as Vallejo did — "I shall die," and then supply the details of our own anticipated death.

WHEN I GO

Karen Silsby

Wild Women Writing Workshop (2008)

I shall die like a shrewd hawk, bent to the wind, stalwart, and gaining height.

I shall die like the sparrow, twittering a song of remembrance.

I shall die like a crow, cawing about this and that.

I shall die like an owl, grown wise by her night haunts.

I shall die like Ana's hummingbird, flitting and twitting over a job half-done.

I shall die like an old robin, yanking my brazen dinner out of the oven.

I shall die like a cardinal, beautifully enrobed.

I shall die like all birds, who have wintered and weathered.

And, I shall die for the new generation, in order that they might live, long and full.

EXPLORATION: Considering Death

What are your fantasies about your own death? Does it frighten you to imagine it? Or do you find it intriguing?

Have you imagined what people might say at your funeral or which folks might attend? Dian said of a person who had recently died, "I think she wrote her own obituary; nobody else would write it that edgy."

Have you created a will, including what you'd like done with your body after your physical death? Have you considered how death will come for you?

IF DEATH WERE A WOMAN

Ellen Kort

I'd want her to come for me smelling of cinnamon
wearing bright cotton purple maybe hot pink

a red bandana in her hair She'd bring
good coffee papaya juice bouquet of sea grass

saltine crackers and a lottery ticket We'd dip
our fingers into moist pouches of lady's slippers

crouch down to see how cabbages feel when wind
bumps against them in the garden We'd walk

through Martin's woods find the old house
its crumbling foundation strung with honeysuckle vines

and in the front yard a surprise jonquils
turning the air yellow glistening and ripe

still blooming for a gardener long gone
We'd head for the beach wearing strings of shells

around our left ankles laugh at their ticking
sounds the measured beat that comes with dancing

on hard-packed sand the applause of ocean and gulls
She'd play ocarina songs to a moon almost full

and I'd sing off-key We'd glide and swoop
become confetti of leaf fall all wings

floating on small whirlwinds never once dreading
the heart-silenced drop And when it was time

she would not bathe me instead we'd scrub the porch
pour leftover water on flowers stand a long time

in the sun and silence then holding hands
we'd pose for pictures in the last light

Set aside a long writing time, an hour or more, and respond
to some of the questions above in freewrite sessions. Write in
different POVs — first person, "I," second person, "you," and
third person, "she" or your name. Notice how each change in
point of view brings you nearer or distances you from your
emotional response to the writing.

Life and Loss, Grief and Mourning

Rare is the person who has not witnessed or participated in
funeral or memorial services. Ceremonies surrounding death
are ancient and many, each with their own rituals. Whatever
culture or religion they hail from, and whether they are public
or private, these rites help us recognize the reality of the death
and allow us to feel the pain of our loss and to mourn. The
pause we take to acknowledge death and remember the person
who died also gives us the time to ask the deeper questions and
to search for meaning.

In our own lives, we experience many deaths and losses
that we may not mark with ceremonies or rituals. Not the death
of another human being, but the death of a dream, the loss of a
relationship, the burning down of a home or a move away from
a place we love. Life is as crowded with losses, large and small,
as a mountain stream is strewn with stones. If we don't grieve
and leave these losses along the way, we must carry them with
us forever, like those stones, weighing us down.

In *Thinking about Memoir*, Abigail Thomas wrote, "I don't
believe that everything happens for a reason, but I have faith in

our ability to retrieve from loss something valuable to keep, or to give away." Again, we're directed to write.

EXPLORATION: Weaving the Thread of Loss

So many losses in our lives: roads not taken, lost opportunities, the loss of friends and relationships. Lost things, lost objects, lost "stuff." I once left a lambskin rug I'd brought back from New Zealand at an apartment I moved from decades ago. Compared to the loss of a deep friendship, this loss may seem trivial, but I still long for the feel of my bare feet against that wool, and where such longing remains after so many years, surely something deeper lies beneath the surface.

This Exploration asks you to write the stories of your losses, to acknowledge them, no matter how great or small. If you remember the loss, it has meaning, and who can say from what comes the deeper pain.

As you're writing about one loss, another may appear. If this happens, make a note in your Journey Notes so you won't forget, and continue on with your original story. You'll have time to write the next and the next and the next.

By writing its story, you acknowledge your loss; writing about it is a way of mourning it. Writing, like weeping, is a way of releasing of what needs to be released.

Legacies Made, Legacies Left

After the death of her aunt, my friend Joan traveled back to New England to attend to her affairs. In going through boxes in the dusty attic of the home where her aunt lived for many years, Joan came upon a diary kept by her grandmother. The book was filled with the quotidian — who came to Sunday dinner, the tree that lost a limb to lightning. For Joan, though, it was as if she'd found the proverbial pearl of great value. Through the notes in the journal, Joan discovered details about her grandmother she'd never known, the small things that made up her daily life, how she lived, and what she cared about. Her grandmother's life took on depth and nuance, a singular, individual life revealed through the sometimes offhand notations in a diary. Such can be the effect of our stories as legacy.

I have been a journal keeper since I received my first diary with its tiny lock and key. As I previously noted, at one point in my early twenties, I burned them all. But still I write, daily and sometimes more often than that, filling one new journal after another. Now, each month when I pay for my storage unit where boxes of these old journals languish, and as I add another and another to my bookshelves at home, heavy with my ponderings and banal with my to-do lists, I wonder if I should continue to keep them. To what end? Do I imagine them a legacy of a sort?

I received this note from Drusilla:

Several years ago, I made a decision not to destroy the journals I wrote when I was in my twenties, thirties, and forties. I don't really expect my children or grandchildren to read them, but you never know.

I decided to save them because of something that happened to a friend of mine. I'll call her Leigh, her mother Dorothy. Dorothy was a concert artist of extraordinary talent. She was also bipolar and had a love-hate relationship with the piano, her husband, and her life. When she died, she left more than a dozen large journals, which her psychoanalyst had instructed her to write in every day.

After her mother's death, Leigh found the writings so disturbing that she destroyed them after just a few pages. When she heard this, my own mother was terribly sad. I'll never forget what she said. "Poor Dorothy. Now no one will ever really know her."

So if my kids want to really, truly know me, the wild me, they are welcome to my journals. It's all there. If they'd rather not, that's okay, too. After so long, I know me. That's most important.

Legacies are what we leave behind; they serve as a kind of witness to our lives. They are not always tangible like journals, or art we've created, or books or poems we've written, or heirlooms, or collections. We may leave endowments or trusts, businesses we've owned or organizations we started, but to so many of the women I asked, more important and meaningful are the intangibles: love we've given, kindnesses we've shared. Love and children and love and family, love and love and love was mentioned again and again in their generous responses to my questions, and the hope that the way they've led their lives will be valued.

"When comes my time," Victoria wrote, "I hope I've shown my children strength and integrity. And a willingness to follow the spark within to rebuild and flourish after it all falls apart."

Their lists included tangibles, too:

A legacy of pancakes with syrup or savory ones with gravy...gadgets and animals and a working farm...a well-used trampoline and many games; some artworks, some songs, some stories and poems, and a metal piggy-bank in the shape of a corner mailbox; my art, my heart, and the "good china" left to me by generations of women before me; books I have written and films I have helped create; my myriad journals that I hope will be read and acknowledged by my grandkids...

Notebooks and poems and scraps of funky art. Books. Glass doorknobs. Bird nests; stories, the ones I write as songs; the work I've done with women; things I have created: jewelry, journals full of blind drawings, episodes of "Christian Crafternoon," and the ultimate creation — my son Jimmy.

And again — love and family. "Let it be said that I really, really love."

Our legacy is of the past, but it is of the future, too. Legacies are a way of continuing. I have often spoken about creating a ceremony on Arbor Day to plant a tree in recognition and acknowledgment of all the paper we writers use. I would name it a PoetTree and hope that one day other writers might sit beneath its shade and write.

EXPLORATION: Legacies of a Life Lived Soulfully

In *The Need for Roots* Simone Weil wrote, "To be rooted is perhaps the most important and least recognized need of the human soul. To be able to give, one has to possess, and we possess no other life, no other living sap, than the treasures stored up from the past and digested, assimilated and created afresh by us."

When your time comes, what will you leave behind — the good china or something of your wild, authentic self? Writing about your legacy provides an opportunity for you to speak of what has mattered to you in this life, and what you hope will live on after you die.

If your thoughts go to list making, let the list be the beginning of deeper work, exploring what each treasure has meant to you.

But before I Die...

Sprawled along an outside wall of a funky bar in a San Diego neighborhood is a giant chalkboard with the heading "Before I die I want to _____." I'd often walked by and read what people wrote in the spaces provided below the evocative headline, but I'd never taken the time to fill in the blank myself until one October day when my daughter and her father were visiting. We'd stopped for coffee at the café across the street, and as we sat on the patio and people-watched, Amy asked if I'd written my "Before I die I want to _____" yet. When I confessed that I had not, she said, "Let's do it."

We wandered along the sidewalk, reading what other people had written: "Get married," "Skydive," "Know God," "Sleep with Jeffrey." Line after chalked line of human wishes and longings, some touching, some whimsical, some improbable, and some invitingly simple.

> **NOTES FOR NURTURING WILD VOICE**
>
> • Celebrate your voice. It's your gift, to receive and to give.
> • Do it all again.

Amy's dad filled in his blank and Amy hers, but I dawdled, indecisive, even a little shy. The writings are anonymous, but still my daughter and my first husband would be witness to my public confession. Also I considered this statement somehow significant. I'd just celebrated one of those decade birthdays and may have been a little sensitive about my mortality. Certainly my Libran indecision was playing its familiar part. Then again, it could have been my perfectionism messing with my wild voice.

Finally, squeezing the worn-down nub of a violet-colored piece of chalk, I filled in the blank: "Before I die I want to fall in love again."

There. That felt true.

The "Before I Die" walls are the conception of artist Candy Chang, who created the first one on the side of a devastated building in New Orleans in 2011. At this writing, there are five hundred such walls in the United States and sixty-five other countries, with messages written in thirty languages. Perhaps there's such a wall in your town. You can find out more about Candy Chang and the "Before I Die" public art project and a recently published book at beforeidie.cc.

EXPLORATION: Before I Die...

This Exploration asks you to consider your deepest longings as well as to note the simple things that can bring beauty and pleasure to your life.

What is important to you? What matters? How do you want to lead your life? Spend your today?

Elisabeth Kübler-Ross said, "It's only when we truly know and understand that we have a limited time on earth — and that we have no way of knowing when our time is up — that we will begin to live each day to the fullest, as if it was the only one we had."

Rather than filling just a single blank line in your Journey Notes, take as long as you want to write.

Continuing the Journey:
Further Explorations into Death, Loss, and Legacies

1. My Uncle Harvey died a year or so ago, the last family member of my mother and father's generation to die. I remember thinking that he was the final adult witness to my sisters' and my early childhood. There would be no more stories of that time. "Stories have to be told or they die and when they die, we can't remember who we are or why we're here," writes Sue Monk Kidd.

    What stories must you tell before they will be lost forever?

2. Not all deaths are physical. Think of the life/death/life cycle, or the idea in folktales and in all nature, that for something to be born, something else must die. Sometimes we experience a crisis that may feel like a death, but out of what may appear a disaster comes a shining new life. What have you experienced that follows the life/death/life cycle?

3. My friend Amy posts obituaries she finds interesting on her Facebook page, and another friend collects epitaphs, those commemorative sayings inscribed on gravestones. (*Excuse my dust* — Dorothy Parker; *Called back* — Emily Dickinson; *Against you I will fling myself unvanquished and unyielding, O Death!* —Virginia Woolf.)

    Give your wild voice the opportunity to write an elegy for you, or write your own obituary or epitaph.

4. When my sisters and I were young girls, our mother joined a children's classic book club, an expense I expect was a

sacrifice for her in those days. This gift from my mother was the beginning of my lifelong love of reading and the pleasure I continue to derive from the physical presence of books. This is her legacy to me.

What has been left to you as a legacy?

5. Throughout our lives we gather and collect, keep and hold and treasure and get rid of and move on. We experience and reexperience and return to a place or a time or a person so that we can attempt to capture again what we loved. We witness and praise and applaud, we taste and eat and drink, we remember and forget and remember again. Write what you will miss when you die.

Notes from the Journey

1. Your Journey Notes book may be looking a bit ragged these days; you've been writing in it and carrying it around with you for some time. You may even be on your second or third journal by now. I hope you have filled them with many stories — some that you thought you'd forgotten, some that surprised you, some you've been intending to write for a long, long time. I hope the sound of your wild voice comes more naturally to you now and that you like the noise it makes. Read back through some of your pages and notice when you've written your authentic wildness.

2. As you've gone through this chapter, were you aware of your physical responses? Even as I wrote some of the material, I felt that familiar walnut of grief in my throat, sometimes I became aware that I was holding my breath, and once, when I was writing about my sister, I found myself in tears. I was glad to cry again for my sister. "Tears are a river that take you someplace," Dr. Estés wrote. I hope you

allowed some tears to carry you as you did the deep work this chapter asks of you.

3. If there is a "Before I Die" wall in your community, you may want to visit it and take the waiting chalk in your own hand to fill in the blank. If there isn't a wall, maybe you and your Wild Women pack will consider making one or spurring a local organization to take the project on.

EPILOGUE
The Road Home

Every word a woman writes changes the story of the world, revises the official version.

— Carolyn See

Something of the wild knows its way home — the songbird finds its way back to the warmth, the rabbit scurries through the trail-marked brush, the flower turns its face to the sun, and our own wild nature shows us the road home to Self.

This journey we have taken through the canyons and arroyos of our lives has given us a language we now speak as our native tongue. On our journey we have tasted memories, sweet and bitter; smelled our own blood; laid our hands upon the stones of our history and felt its warmth and its chill. We have seen the curve of our bones, and the shape of our shadow silhouetted against the light. Our wild voice has filled our ears with deep song and perhaps caused our fingers to tremble with truth as we wrote our stories. And now we come home, a resting place.

"It is said that all you are seeking is also seeking you, that if you lie still, sit still, it will find you. Once it is here, don't move away. Rest. See what happens next," wrote Clarissa Pinkola Estés.

This is the place we find ourselves. This now. This moment. Tired, maybe, from the journey, but refreshed, too. Emboldened with a deeper understanding of ourselves as Wild Women, and fluent in the language of our wild voice.

The stories that arose from a place of authenticity and written in your wild voice will continue their echo. As in the Carolyn See quote above, you have, through your writing, changed the story of the world. In the work you've done, you've changed, too, though you may not be able to say exactly how. When you see your image in the mirror, you may, at first glance, appear the same, but looking more closely, holding the steady gaze of your eyes, you'll know. Others may notice, too. "Have you changed your hair?" they might ask. "Something's different about you."

And still, there are so many more stories to tell, more memories to explore, more life to give voice to. Phrases and images scattered throughout your Journey Notes will call, sometimes at the oddest hour. You'll see a stranger in the supermarket and be reminded of a poem you started weeks before; a night bird's call will wake you and send you to your writing desk to respond with your own wild song. Your senses, keenly attuned to your wild nature, will demand response. You have so much more to say, so much more writing to do.

And so, once again, I light the candle on my table and set my stones nearby, where the candlelight reflects their polished surfaces. This morning's Tarot card, a perfect message for the days' work, reads "Moment to Moment" and shows the image of a smiling figure skipping along stones in a river, sure-footed and balanced, the colors of the rainbow surrounding him.

In the last moments of the final meeting of our Wild Women writing workshops, just before we extinguish our candle for the final time, I read a meditation that takes us on a journey back through the work we have done over our time together. After some moments of silence, we turn once again to our notebooks and respond to what comes to us intuitively. Often the writing finds voice in the form of a poem or its own meditation.

Take time now to be still, and let all you have written over this time, all your Explorations, all your lists and stories and poems and word sketches, settle around you. Close your eyes and let what is seeking you in this moment find you. Allow the images, colors, and sounds to fill you. Listen for the voice of your authentic wildness. You will know what to say. The words will once again find their way onto the page, and once again, the story of the world will change.

APPENDIX
Call of the Wild
The Making of a Wild Women Writing Group

For more than two decades I've been writing in Wild Women writing workshops and with groups of Wild Women on Full Moon Retreats and around the tables on many a hot summer night. No matter where or how we come together, from the flare of the first candle lighting to its final extinguishing hours, days, or weeks later, I always know I've been a part of something extraordinary and that, as a result, I have been changed. In these circles of like-spirited women, my voice has been heard and my stories written. Not all of them, mind you; that will take a lifetime, but the stories that were coaxed or seduced or came exploding onto the page during our time together.

The ones that stay with me long after the last glow of candlelight fades, the ones I hear again and again in my head and remember how they and the women who wrote them affected us. How moved we were when Laurinda wrote about her grandmother's madness, how we laughed at Katie's story of that wild night she made love on the platform of a billboard above the interstate, and the sigh that stayed in the air following Jo's reading of the piece she written to the prompt "what I'll miss when I die." I remember how, again and again, we sat in the holy silence that descends when writing touches that deep place inside and marks us forever.

Tears, laughter, memories, shared and private; creative bursts followed by stillness deep as midnight; connections heart to heart, wild mind to wild mind; and more than a few spontaneous howls — all this and more can happen when Wild Women join in spirit and in community and share their stories. I hope you'll be inspired to create your own Wild Women writing group.

Let this book be your guide and provide a map for your journey into Wild Woman territory. Consider it an adventure, one suitable for your wild nature. Is it risky? Maybe, a little.

You may wonder what it will be like, being in a group of other women who all claim the identity "wild." Is my wild the same as their wild? Maybe I'm thinking stalking the moon in the midnight woods and they're thinking Saturday night in Vegas with a few daiquiris and the Chippendales. My wild voice might be set to howl, while theirs is all, "Yahoo!"

This is what I know: any given mix of Wild Women will create its own many-voiced choir, and nobody can say what new sound might be made or how the harmonies might blend. That's part of the magic and one of the reasons I keep doing it. Besides, we Wild Women thrive on risk. And you might expand on the opportunities for finding new tones and ranges for your own wild voice by joining together with a pack of like-spirited women.

Calling the Circle

Start by sniffing the air. You probably already know women like yourself, women you recognize by their wild nature — that twitch of ear, a muddy print — who also like to write. You don't have to identify yourself as "writer" to be part of a Wild Women writing group. The only requirement is a desire to write your stories from a deep and authentic voice, and the willingness to commit to the group.

Decide how public or how private you want to make your group. How wide do you want to open your doors? How large do you want the group to be?

Where will the group meet? If yours is an open group, you may want to find a public place to meet, the community room at a library or a separate room in a café. The space needs to feel safe for women to read aloud what they've written. If your group is made up of friends and women who know one another, then a private home can be a warm and welcoming place that invites the kind of intimacy that often develops in Wild Women groups.

Do you want to work through the chapters in the book in thirteen weekly sessions, or do one chapter a month for a year-long commitment, or some other configuration of your own creation?

It's not unusual for women to drop out of the group over the course of your time together. Some decide the work isn't for them; some get scared at their own wildness and retreat to safer ground. Maybe they'll return, maybe not. For others, life interferes and they're unable to keep to their commitment. I like to check in with those who go missing, just to let them know they're always welcome and that I understand if they can't continue.

Structuring the Meetings

Leaders: The leader maintains the supportive and respectful atmosphere of the meetings and generally keeps the wild within bounds (except during the writing, when wild is encouraged). She keeps an eye on the clock, so meetings begin and end on time, and facilitates discussions so that everyone is included. She doesn't control, and she doesn't "fix" anyone.

She encourages laughter and allows space for tears. She knows when to hold the silence and when to initiate movement.

I've been in groups where leadership rotates through the membership, I've led many a group, and I've been participant in groups led by others, and I've enjoyed them all. I like the element of surprise when I'm participant and don't know what journey the leader will take us on. I like the variety of the different styles of facilitating when leadership rotates through the group and the wonderful display of creativity each woman brings to that role. And, as leader, I like creating a meeting that I think will provide a stimulating and evocative experience for others.

Open: By now you know that I like the ceremony of lighting candles to begin my writing groups and my own writing sessions. For me, lighting the candle signals the formal beginning to a special occasion; it provides a focus of attention and a settling in. You can also begin the meeting with reading a poem or a set of guidelines the group has adopted or by ringing a chime. Observing a moment of silence will also bring group members present and into the circle.

Check-in: Each member places on the table the item or memento she has brought as representative for her of that chapter's focus. Check-in time is also an opportunity for each member to take a few minutes to talk about her experience with the work during the previous week or month.

Content: Obviously a meeting time of two or three hours won't allow for working through all the material in each chapter and writing to each Exploration. Members should read the chapter prior to the meeting. Material to be covered and Explorations to be written to can be determined in advance by the leader, or members can suggest or vote for their preferences.

Writing to other Explorations in the chapter can be done outside the group, alone, or with other members in informal sessions — an hour together at a café or in someone's home. Just sitting across a table from another writer can help get the pen moving. My happy experience is that writing partners sometimes find each other during the course of a group.

Writing and Reading

Some of the Explorations include a suggested length of time for writing, but these are just suggestions. During a two- or three-hour meeting, the time given for each writing will necessarily need to be contained. It's not unusual for writers to be unable to get down all they wanted to say in a timed-writing session. I generally give a two-minute notice before the end of each writing session and encourage writers not to be in so much of a hurry to get to an end that they skim over the deeper, richer stuff. You can come back and finish it later, I tell them.

Always allow time for reading aloud after each of the written Explorations. Depending on the size of your group, everyone may not be able to read each time, nor will they want to, but each writer should have the opportunity to read at least one time during the meeting. No one is required to read her work aloud, though sometimes a little friendly encouragement will help a shy writer give voice to her words.

No critique is ever given on the writing, though brief comments or responses may be offered. Our job is not to fix anyone's raw, first-draft writing but to listen closely and offer our silent support as the work is being read. And though we may sometimes want to and often can hardly contain ourselves, I don't encourage applause; the readings aren't performance. They give us an opportunity to hear our work aloud.

Closing: Just as we formally opened the meeting, so, too, should we formally close it. Our attention to this ritual continues to lend reverence to the work that is being done and respects the intention of the group. Conclude with a quote, a poem, a moment of silence, the ringing of a chime, or maybe a howl! Finally, extinguish the candle, which releases the energy and signals completion.

Celebrating the Work: Wild Voices in Print and Out Loud

At the conclusion of every Wild Women writing workshop, I invite members to select two or three pieces they've written over the course of our time together to submit for the creation of a chapbook. (A chapbook is a small booklet, usually 8 ½ x 11, folded in half and stapled, with a limited number of pages.) When the pieces are revised and edited (I set a word-count limit), they're assembled into the book. Copies are made, and a date is set and a place selected for a reading. Friends and family, and even the public, are invited, and all the brave and beautiful Wild Women come together to read some of their work aloud. Now comes the applause part.

You can find out more about creating a chapbook at many online sites including Poets & Writers (pw.org/content/diy _how_to_make_and_bind_chapbooks).

I'm always a little sad at the end of any group, sad and nostalgic and also grateful for the time we had together and the community we shared. I count among my friends some of the Wild Women who've been in the groups, a few of whom I still write with even as time has lengthened our teeth and thinned our coats. The fierceness has not diminished, the passion has not faded, and we still get our howl on. I wish the same for you.

ACKNOWLEDGMENTS

Who can say when an idea will become manifest — when the stars align? when the weather turns? when the student is ready? I can't explain what happened, but some mysterious and powerful force took hold at summer's end, 2013, and next thing I knew I was writing the book that had been in my mind and heart for a decade. For whatever magic was afoot that allowed this to happen, I am grateful.

There is other magic afoot, and it is not so mysterious. Georgia Hughes, editorial director at New World Library, and an editor I have been privileged to work with and learn from previously and whose practical and intuitive knowledge I value and trust, once again advised, suggested, and guided me through the process. Because of her expertise and sensibilities, the book is sleeker, stronger, and more of what it wanted to be.

I am honored to have another book published by New World Library, a publishing house that, for so many years, has brought books of beauty and vision to the world. My gratitude toward and applause for the talented, creative professionals who make these books possible. Thank you, Tracy Cunningham, for the gorgeous cover design and for your patience in finding just the right image that expresses the spirit of this book. Grateful appreciation also to Kristen Cashman; Tona Pearce Myers, who designed the book's beautiful interior; Jonathan Wichmann; and Ami Parkerson. Thank you, Munro Magruder and Monique Muhlenkamp and Kim Corbin. My thanks also to copy editor Mimi Kusch for her careful and thorough work.

The Wild Women writing workshops were originally inspired by Clarissa Pinkola Estés's work, particularly *Women Who Run with the Wolves*. Thank you, Dr. Estés, for arousing the wild in us. And thank you to all the Wild Women who've been a part of the workshops. This book is a result of your lively, authentic, and open-hearted participation, and I'm pleased that some of the writing from our groups found its way into the book. Deep gratitude also to the Wild Women who responded so generously and honestly to my queries and for allowing me to use your words and your experiences.

Thanks go to my friends, writing and otherwise, who make my life richer and my writing better. I wish I could list all your names here.

Thanks to my students and to the participants in my groups and workshops, and especially to members of the Wednesday Writing Group for your good humor and patience with my erratic schedule over the past year as this book took shape.

I am grateful to my family and for their understanding and acceptance and generosity of heart — thank you, Chris and Stephanie, Alex and Andrew, Jackson and Craig, my darling Amy and Kathleen, and Mike and Matt, the grandsons I don't see often enough. You are part of this book, Sharon, in memories and in stories.

There are so many ways I am grateful to Jill Hall — for her generous support and solid advice, time writing together, retreats at the J&J Ranch, where creativity is nurtured and nature is honored. Thank you, Ellen Yaffa, for the time spent writing alone/together. Thank you, Roger Aplon, for your steadfast belief in me and my work and for your poetry, which always inspires me. Steve Montgomery, my Thursday Writers cohort and great good friend: I am indebted to you for your research expertise and in so many other ways. You know my secrets, which you keep, and my dreams, which you encourage. I am eternally grateful for both.

Once again, Dian Greenwood, you've walked with me, laughed with me, listened to me, encouraged me, and humored me through another book; I couldn't do it without you. Camille Soleil, you're ever-present in my heart and in every word I write. My prayer was that Drusilla Campbell would be able to hold this book in her hands and read of my gratitude for our deep and long friendship. But this was not to be. Rest in peace, my dear friend.

NOTES

Introduction

1 *No matter by which culture:* Clarissa Pinkola Estés, *Women Who Run with the Wolves: Myths and Stories of the Wild Woman Archetype* (New York: Ballantine, 1992), 6.

One: Maps for the Journey

9 *The fact is that anybody who has survived childhood:* Flannery O'Connor, *Mystery and Manners: Occasional Prose* (New York: Farrar, Straus and Giroux, 1969), 84.

13 *Occasionally the river floods in these places:* Toni Morrison, "The Site of Memory," in *What Moves at the Margin: Selected Nonfiction,* ed. Carolyn Denard (Jackson, MS: University of Mississippi Press, 2008), 77.

14 *Even the shape of my writing:* Julia Cameron, *Walking in This World: The Practical Art of Creativity* (New York: Tarcher/Penguin, 2003), 8.

14 *The typewriter separated me:* Rita Guibert, "The Art of Poetry No. 14," *The Paris Review,* interview with Pablo Neruda, www.the parisreview.org/interviews/4091/the-art-of-poetry-no-14-pablo -neruda.

16 *Loneliness is the poverty of self:* May Sarton, *Mrs. Stevens Hears the Mermaids Singing* (New York: Norton, 1975), 183.

18 *Symbols are the living mirrors:* Mark Nepo, *The Book of Awakening: Having the Life You Want by Being Present to the Life You Have* (San Francisco: Conari, 2000), 89.

Two: Claiming Wild Woman

22 *Through sights of great beauty:* Clarissa Pinkola Estés, *Women Who Run with the Wolves: Myths and Stories of the Wild Woman Archetype* (New York: Ballantine, 1992), 7.

23 *Ghosty from neglect:* Estés, *Women Who Run*, 7.

23 *Memory thick as mud:* Janet Fitch, *White Oleander* (New York: Little, Brown, 1999), 76.

30 *A name should be taken as an act:* Erica Jong, *Fear of Fifty: A Midlife Memoir* (New York: HarperCollins, 1994; repr., Tarcher, 2006), 139.

31 *My real name is:* Susan G. Wooldridge, *Poemcrazy: Freeing Your Life with Words* (New York: Clarkson Potter, 1996), 38.

33 *For some women air, night, sunlight:* Estés, *Women Who Run*, 196.

Three: Wild Child, Wild Girl

40 *Childhood is the first, inescapable political situation:* Quoted in Felicia R. Lee, "Survivor with the Eyes of a Child," *New York Times*, July 4, 2000, www.nytimes.com/2000/07/04/books/a-feminist-survivor-with-the-eyes-of-a-child.html.

40 *Wash the white clothes:* Jamaica Kincaid, "Girl," in *At the Bottom of the River* (New York: Farrar, Straus and Giroux, 1983), 3.

42 *All the medicine people knew:* Luis Urrea, *The Hummingbird's Daughter* (New York: Little, Brown, 2006), 198.

46 *When we were sixteen:* Dorianne Laux, "Rites of Passage," in *Girls Like Us*, ed. Gina Misiroglu (Novato, CA: New World Library, 1999), 144.

47 *Stories that needed to be told:* Clarissa Pinkola Estés, *Women Who Run with the Wolves: Myths and Stories of the Wild Woman Archetype* (New York: Ballantine, 1992), 5.

48 *It's OK to repeat:* Kathleen Adams, *Journey to the Self: Twenty-Two Paths to Personal Growth* (New York: Warner, 1990), 125.

Four: Body Writing

51 *Landscape of truth-telling:* Linda Hogan, "Department of the Interior," in *Minding the Body: Women Writers on Body and Soul,* ed. Patricia Foster (New York: Doubleday, 1994), 166–67.

52 *Most people think of the mind:* Diane Ackerman, *A Natural History of the Senses* (New York: Random House, 1990), xix.

58 *I sing the body electric:* Walt Whitman, "I Sing the Body Electric," in *Leaves of Grass* (New York: Bantam Classic, 2004), 79.

58 *I dote on myself, there is that lot of me:* Whitman, "Song of Myself," in *Leaves of Grass,* 22.

59 *In a foghorn-like blast:* Mary Karr, "The Hot Dark," *The New Yorker* (Sept. 4, 2000): 42, www.newyorker.com/magazine/2000/09/04/the-hot-dark.

59 *The wholesome good looks of the nice one:* Rebecca Mead, "Eerily Composed: Nico Muhly's Sonic Magic," *The New Yorker* (Feb. 11, 2008), www.newyorker.com/magazine/2008/02/11/eerily-composed.

59 *He moves delicately:* Larissa MacFarquhar, "The Bench Burner," *The New Yorker* (Dec. 10, 2001): 78, www.newyorker.com/magazine/2001/12/10/the-bench-burner.

59 *She wore her usual Betty Grable hairdo:* Margaret Atwood, *The Edible Woman* (New York: Anchor, 1998), 11–12.

61 *The act of writing creatively:* John Fox, "Words from the Marrow," in *The Soul of Creativity: Insights into the Creative Process,* ed. Tona Pearce Myers (Novato, CA: New World Library, 1999), 137.

63 *Atwood responded:* Margaret Atwood, "The Female Body," *Michigan Quarterly Review* 29, no. 24: 490–93, quod.lib.umich.edu/m/mqrarchive/act2080.0029.004/17:3?g=mqrg;rgn=full+text;view=image;xc=1.

64 *To write "my body" plunges me:* Adrienne Rich, "Notes Toward a Politics of Location," in *Blood, Bread, and Poetry: Selected Prose 1979–1985* (New York: Norton, 1994), 215.

65 *As though you were creating an "owner's manual":* SARK, *Succulent Wild Woman* (New York: Simon & Schuster, 1997), 77.

65 *Color in nature images:* Tina Welling, *Writing Wild: Forming a Creative Partnership with Nature* (Novato, CA: New World Library, 2014), 90.

Five: Family

67 *[Family] is the nest:* Thomas Moore, *Care of the Soul: A Guide for Cultivating Depth and Sacredness in Everyday Life* (New York: HarperCollins, 1992), 28.

69 *To be intimately acquainted with people:* Kendall Hailey, *The Day I Became an Autodidact and the Advice, Adventures, and Acrimonies That Befell Me Thereafter* (New York: Delta, 1988), 3–4.

71 *We received our coloring from Norsemen:* Janet Fitch, *White Oleander* (New York: Little, Brown, 1994), 4.

71 *Stimulate the mythic imagination:* Deena Metzger, *Writing for Your Life: Discovering the Story of Your Life's Journey* (San Francisco: HarperSanFrancisco, 1992), 170.

74 *My mother was an upright piano:* Tania Hershman, "My Mother Was an Upright Piano," in *My Mother Was an Upright Piano: Fictions* (Bristol, UK: Tangent, 2012), 109–10.

78 *A daughter's relationship with her mother:* Victoria Secunda, *Women and Their Fathers: The Sexual and Romantic Impact of the First Man in Your Life* (New York: Delacorte, 1992), 54.

78 *Out of the corner of one eye:* Jamaica Kincaid, *Annie John* (New York: Macmillan, 1985), 106–7.

78 *The deepest mutuality:* Adrienne Rich, *Of Woman Born: Motherhood as Experience and Institution* (New York: Norton, 1986), 226.

79 *It is hard to write about my own mother:* Rich, *Of Woman Born,* 221.

81 *A Saturday, in January:* Carol Lucci Wisner, "Stonehenge and the Louvre Were Cool," in *In Short: A Collection of Brief Creative Nonfiction,* ed. Judith Kitchen and Mary Paumier Jones (New York: Norton, 1996), 256–57.

84 *It doesn't matter who my father was:* Anne Sexton, "The Poet's Story," in *A Small Journal,* ed. Howard Moss (New York: Macmillan, 1973), entry for January 1, 1973.

84 *These are the snapshots of marriage:* Anne Sexton, "All My Pretty

Ones," in *The Complete Poems of Anne Sexton* (Boston: Houghton Mifflin, 1981).

Six: Writing Place

89 *We can't separate who we are:* Sam Keen and Anne Valley-Fox, *Your Mythic Journey: Finding Meaning in Your Life through Writing and Storytelling* (Los Angeles: Tarcher, 1973), 44.

91 *Whether they are in Malaysia:* Linda Hogan, "Walking," in *Dwellings: A Spiritual History of the Living World* (New York: Norton, 1995), 157.

92 *There are occasions when you can hear:* John Hay, quoted in Hogan, "Walking," 157–58.

93 *Location is the crossroads:* Eudora Welty, "Place in Fiction," in *Eye of the Story: Selected Essays and Reviews* (New York: Vintage, 1990), 118.

94 *We do not say simply "The Hanging Gardens":* Welty, "Place in Fiction," 119.

95 *My wound is geography:* Pat Conroy, *The Prince of Tides* (Boston: Houghton Mifflin Company, 1986), 1.

96 *It is true that a country encapsulates:* Edna O'Brien, "Escape to England," in *QPB Anthology of Women's Writing*, ed. Susan Cahill (New York: Quality Paperback Book Club, 2002), 501.

97 *The catalyst that converts:* Alan Gussow, "A Sense of Place," in *The Earth Speaks*, ed. Steve Van Matre and Bill Weiler (Warrenville, IL: The Institute for Earth Education, 1983), 45.

102 *Every man, every woman, carries:* Edward Abbey, *Desert Solitaire: A Season in the Wilderness* (New York: Ballantine, 1985), 1.

104 *He who cannot howl:* Charles Simic, "Ax," in *Five Blind Men* (Freemont, MI: Sumac, 1969), 51.

Seven: Loves and Lovers

105 *Speak to us of love:* Kahlil Gibran, *The Prophet* (Auckland, New Zealand: Floating Press, 2008), 12.

107 *And why do people want to be in love?:* As quoted in Jonathan Cott, *Susan Sontag: The Complete Rolling Stone Interview* (New Haven, CT: Yale University Press, 2013), 100.

107 *Oh, gallant was the first love:* Dorothy Parker, "Pictures in the Smoke" from *Enough Rope (Poems)* in *The Portable Dorothy Parker* (New York: Penguin Books, 1976), 115.

109 *What lips my lips have kissed:* Edna St. Vincent Millay, "What My Lips Have Kissed," in *Collected Poems* (New York: Harper & Row, 1956).

112 *The true liberation of eroticism:* Anaïs Nin, *In Favor of the Sensitive Man and Other Essays* (San Diego: Harcourt Brace Jovanovich, 1976), 11.

112 *We have, first of all:* Nin, *In Favor,* 11.

112 *Yes and how he kissed me:* James Joyce, *Ulysses: The Corrected Text* (New York: Vintage, 1986), 641–42.

114 *The most erotic scene:* Carol Shields, interview with Elizabeth Benedict, in Benedict, *The Joy of Writing Sex: A Guide for Fiction Writers* (Cincinnati, OH: Story Press, 1996), 16.

114 *I thought I might try to write:* Shields, interview, 16.

115 *First thought, best thought:* Collected by Allen Ginsberg in his "Mind Writing Slogans," www.poetspath.com/transmissions/messages/ginsberg.html.

118 *It is not only necessary to love:* Michelle Lovric, ed., *Love Letters: An Anthology of Passion* (New York: Shooting Star Press, 1994), front cover.

Eight: Friends and Companions

122 *For instance, in what's called the landmark:* "UCLA Researchers Identify Key Biobehavioral Pattern Used by Women to Manage Stress," *ScienceDaily* (May 22, 2000), www.sciencedaily.com/releases/2000/05/000522082151.htm).

123 *Another study:* Graham A. Colditz and Susan E. Hankinson, "The Nurses' Health Study: Lifestyle and Health among Women,"

Nature Reviews Cancer 5 (May 2005): 388–96, www.nature.com/nrc/journal/v5/n5/full/nrc1608.html.

124   *For it was in dream:* Toni Morrison, *Sula* (New York: Knopf, 1973), 51.

127   *My memory of Stella:* Katie Roiphe, "Torch Song," in *The Friend Who Got Away: Twenty Women's True Life Tales of Friendships That Blew Up, Burned Out or Faded Away,* ed. Jenny Offill and Elissa Schapell (New York: Doubleday, 2005), 3.

128   *Vita was here for Sunday:* Virginia Woolf, "Diary," in *The Norton Book of Women's Lives,* ed. Phyllis Rose (New York: Norton, 1993), 806.

Nine: Artist/Creator

136   *I would venture to guess:* Virginia Woolf, *A Room of One's Own* (1929; repr., San Diego: Harcourt Brace Jovanovich, 1989), 49.

136   *Out of their own substance: Courage to Change: One Day at a Time in Alanon* (New York: Alanon Family Group, 1992), 67.

136   *Creativity is the work of the heart:* Jan Phillips, *Marry Your Muse: Making a Lasting Commitment to Your Creativity* (Wheaton, IL: Quest Books, 1997), 107.

137   *Had found a jewel down inside:* Zora Neale Hurston, *Their Eyes Were Watching God* (1937; repr., New York: HarperCollins, 1990), 85.

137   *There are many expressions of creativity:* Jean Shinoda Bolen, "Creativity: The Alchemy of Aphrodite," in *The Soul of Creativity: Insights into the Creative Process,* ed. Tona Pearce Myers (Novato, CA: New World Library, 1999), 59.

139   *My first felony:* Sandra Cisneros, *My Wicked, Wicked Ways* (New York: Knopf, 1992), x.

140   *Creativity is interactive:* Bolen, "Creativity," 59.

142   *Your creativity in action is so needed:* SARK, "Make It Real," in *Soul of Creativity,* 39.

144   *This wildness has many faces:* Eric Maisel, *Fearless Creating: A Step-by-Step Guide to Starting and Completing Your Work of Art* (New York: Tarcher/Putnam, 1995), 12.

147   *I chucked the life:* Cisneros, *My Wicked,* x.

Ten: Life Journeys

151 *She was heading up to Slovenia:* Elizabeth Gilbert, *Eat Pray Love*
(New York: Penguin, 2006), 77.

152 *Congratulations! Today is your day:* Dr. Seuss, *Oh, the Places You'll*
Go! (New York: Random House, 1990).

153 *The literature of women's lives:* Phyllis Rose, ed., *The Norton Book of*
Women's Lives (New York: Norton, 1993), 2.

154 *You do not travel if you are afraid:* Ella Maillart, widely quoted on
the Internet.

154 *I'd finally come to understand what it had been:* Cheryl Strayed, *Wild:*
From Lost to Found on the Pacific Crest Trail (New York: Knopf,
2012), 290.

156 *Is there an odyssey the female soul:* Sue Monk Kidd and Ann Kidd
Taylor, *Traveling with Pomegranates: A Mother-Daughter Story*
(New York: Viking, 2009), 6.

156 *You hear a call that cannot be denied:* Elyn Aviva, *Following the*
Milky Way: A Pilgrimage on the Camino de Santiago (Boulder, CO:
Pilgrim's Progress, 2001), xii.

157 *I had grown weary of life in New York:* Mary Morris, *Nothing to*
Declare: Memoirs of a Woman Traveling Alone (New York: Penguin,
1988), 4.

158 *I am intended to be a journeywoman:* Morris, *Nothing,* 23.

160 *So...be your name Buxbaum or Bixby or Bray:* Seuss, *Oh, the Places*
You'll Go!

161 *We travel, initially, to lose ourselves:* Pico Iyer, "Why We Travel,"
Salon.com (March 18, 2000), www.salon.com/2000/03/18/why/.

Eleven: Where the Wild Things Are

164 *Far from frightening, embracing the shadow:* Debbie Ford, introduc-
tion, in Deepak Chopra, Marianne Williamson, and Debbie Ford,
The Shadow Effect: Illuminating the Hidden Power of Your True Self
(New York: HarperCollins, 2011), 3.

165 *Be who you are and will be:* Audre Lorde, "For Each of You," in *From a Land Where Other People Live* (Detroit: Broadside Press, 1973).

174 *Anger is meant to be listened to:* Julia Cameron, *The Artist's Way: A Spiritual Path to Higher Creativity* (New York: Tarcher/Penguin, 1992), 61.

Twelve: Dreams and Synchronicity

178 *One of the most remarkable things:* Clarissa Pinkola Estés, *Women Who Run with the Wolves: Myths and Stories of the Wild Woman Archetype* (New York: Ballantine, 1992), 112.

178 *Albert Einstein called the intuitive mind a sacred gift:* Bob Samples, *The Metaphoric Mind: A Celebration of Creative Consciousness* (Reading, MA: Addison-Wesley, 1976), 26.

178 *It is always with excitement that I wake up:* Jonas Salk, *Anatomy of Reality: Merging of Intuition and Reason* (New York: Columbia University Press, 1983).

179 *If you build it, they will come: Field of Dreams*, directed and screenplay by Phil Alden Robinson, Universal Pictures, 1989; based on the novel *Shoeless Joe* by W. P. Kinsella.

180 *One of the sure ways to know:* Shakti Gawain, "Developing Intuition: Practical Guidance for Daily Life," presentation at Bodhi Tree Bookstore (West Hollywood, CA, 2001), www.bodhitree.com/node/473.

187 *The dream world is the territory:* Deena Metzger, *Writing for Your Life: Discovering the Story of Your Life's Journey* (San Francisco: HarperSanFrancisco, 1992), 221.

187 *Once in the dream of a night:* Sarojini Naidu, "Song of a Dream," in *The Golden Threshold* (New York: John Lane, 1916).

188 *Dreams say what they mean:* Gail Goodwin, *The Finishing School* (1984; repr., New York: Ballantine, 1999), 3.

Thirteen: Death, Loss, and Legacies

194 *Give sorrow words:* William Shakespeare, *Macbeth*, act 4, scene 3, lines 210–11.

195 *After the funeral I pick:* Maxine Kumin, "In Memoriam P.W., Jr., 1921–1980: Retrospect in the Kitchen," in *Our Ground Time Here Will Be Brief* (New York: Viking, 1982).

197 *I shall die in Paris:* César Vallejo, "Black Stone on Top of a White Stone," trans. Thomas Merton, in *In the Dark Before the Dawn: New Selected Poems of Thomas Merton*, ed. Lynn R. Szabo (New York: New Directions, 2005), 233.

198 *I'd want her to come for me smelling of cinnamon:* Ellen Kort, "If Death Were a Woman" in *If Death Were a Woman: Poems* (Milwaukee, WI: Fox Print, 1994).

200 *I don't believe that everything happens:* Abigail Thomas, *Thinking about Memoir* (New York: Sterling, 2008), 81.

204 *To be rooted is perhaps the most important:* Simone Weil, *The Need for Roots: Prelude to a Declaration of Duties Towards Mankind* (London: Routeledge and Kegan Paul, 1952), 40.

206 *It's only when we truly know and understand:* Elisabeth Kübler-Ross, www.ekrfoundation.org/quotes/.

207 *Stories have to be told or they die:* Sue Monk Kidd, *The Secret Life of Bees* (New York: Penguin, 2002), 133.

208 *Tears are a river that take you someplace:* Clarissa Pinkola Estés, *Women Who Run with the Wolves: Myths and Stories of the Wild Woman Archetype* (New York: Ballantine, 1992), 375.

Epilogue: The Road Home

211 *It is said that all you are seeking:* Clarissa Pinkola Estés, *Women Who Run with the Wolves: Myths and Stories of the Wild Woman Archetype* (New York: Ballantine, 1992), 152.

PERMISSION
ACKNOWLEDGMENTS

Grateful acknowledgment is given to the following for permission to reprint quotations in *Wild Women, Wild Voices*. Every effort has been made to contact all rights holders of the material in this book. If notified of errors, the publishers will correct any omissions or mistakes in future editions.

Page 31: "My real name is" from *Poemcrazy: Freeing Your Life with Words* by Susan G. Wooldridge, © 1996 by Susan G. Wooldridge. Used by permission of Crown Books, an imprint of the Crown Publishing Group, a division of Random House LLC. All rights reserved.

Page 46: Dorianne Laux, "Rites of Passage," which appeared in *Girls Like Us: 40 Extraordinary Women Celebrate Girlhood in Story, Poetry, and Song*, ed. Gina Misiroglu, © 1999 by New World Library. Used by permission of the author.

Pages 74–75: Tania Hershman, "My Mother Was an Upright Piano," which appeared in *My Mother Was an Upright Piano: Fictions* by Tania Hershman, © 2012, Tangent Books. Used by permission of the author.

Page 195: Maxine Kumin, "In Memoriam P.W., Jr., 1921–1980: Retrospect in the Kitchen," from *Ground Time Here Will Be Brief* by Maxine Kumin, © 1982 by Maxine Kumin. Viking Adult. Used by permission.

Page 198: Ellen Kort, "If Death Were a Woman," in *If Death Were a Women: Poems* by Ellen Kort, © 1994 by Ellen Kort. Used by permission of the author.

RECOMMENDED READING

Abercrombie, Barbara. *Courage & Craft: Writing Your Life into Story.* Novato, CA: New World Library, 2007.

Ackerman, Diane. *A Natural History of the Senses.* New York: Random House, 1990.

Baldwin, Christina. *Storycatcher: Making Sense of Our Lives through the Power and Practice of Story.* Novato, CA: New World Library, 2005.

Bane, Rosanne. *Dancing in the Dragon's Den: Rekindling the Creative Fire in Your Shadow.* North Beach, ME: Nicolas-Hays, 1999.

Burroway, Janet. *Imaginative Writing: The Elements of Craft,* 4th ed. Boston: Pearson, 2014.

Cahill, Susan, ed. *Writing Women's Lives: An Anthology of Autobiographical Narratives by Twentieth-Century American Women Writers.* New York: Perennial, 1994.

Dillard, Annie. *The Writing Life.* New York: Harper Perennial, 2013.

Estés, Clarissa Pinkola. *Women Who Run with the Wolves: Myths and Stories of the Wild Woman Archetype.* New York: Ballantine, 1992.

Foster, Patricia, ed. *Minding the Body: Women Writers on Body and Soul.* New York: Doubleday, 1994.

Goldberg, Natalie. *Writing Down the Bones: Freeing the Writer Within.* Boston/London: Shambhala, 1986.

Metzger, Deena. *Writing for Your Life: Discovering the Story of Your Life's Journey.* San Francisco: HarperSanFrancisco, 1992.

Misiroglu, Gina, ed. *Girls Like Us: Forty Extraordinary Women Celebrate Girlhood in Story, Poetry, and Song.* Novato, CA: New World Library, 1999.

Myers, Tona Pearce, ed. *The Soul of Creativity: Insights into the Creative Process.* Novato, CA: New World Library, 1999.

Nachmanovitch, Stephen. *Free Play: The Power of Improvisation in Life and the Arts*. New York: Tarcher/Putnam, 1991.

Phillips, Jan. *Marry Your Muse: Making a Lasting Commitment to Your Creativity*. Wheaton, IL: Quest Books, 1997.

Rose, Phyllis, ed. *The Norton Book of Women's Lives*. New York: Norton, 1993.

Shapiro, Dani. *Still Writing: The Perils and Pleasures of a Creative Life*. New York: Grove Press, 2013.

Sher, Gail. *The Intuitive Writer: Listening to Your Own Voice*. New York: Penguin, 2002.

Ueland, Brenda. *If You Want to Write: A Book about Art, Independence and Spirit*, 2nd ed. St. Paul, Graywolf Press, 1987.

Welling, Tina. *Writing Wild: Forming a Creative Partnership with Nature*. Novato, CA: New World Library, 2014.

INDEX

ABOUT THE AUTHOR

Judy Reeves is a writer, teacher, and writing practice provocateur who has written four books on writing, including the award-winning *A Writer's Book of Days*. Her work has appeared in magazines, literary journals, and anthologies, most recently, in *Expressive Writing: Classroom and Community*. She has edited several anthologies and chapbooks, including those born out of her Wild Women writing workshops, which she has led since 1997.

In addition to leading private writing groups, Judy teaches at the University of California–San Diego Extension and at San Diego Writers, Ink, a nonprofit literary organization she cofounded. She also presents workshops at writing conferences and retreats internationally.

Born in the Midwest, Judy has traveled throughout the world but somehow always finds her way back to San Diego, where she lives.

Her website is judyreeveswriter.com, where she blogs as The Lively Muse.

NEW WORLD LIBRARY is dedicated to publishing books and other media that inspire and challenge us to improve the quality of our lives and the world.

We are a socially and environmentally aware company. We recognize that we have an ethical responsibility to our customers, our staff members, and our planet.

We serve our customers by creating the finest publications possible on personal growth, creativity, spirituality, wellness, and other areas of emerging importance. We serve New World Library employees with generous benefits, significant profit sharing, and constant encouragement to pursue their most expansive dreams.

As a member of the Green Press Initiative, we print an increasing number of books with soy-based ink on 100 percent postconsumer-waste recycled paper. Also, we power our offices with solar energy and contribute to non-profit organizations working to make the world a better place for us all.

Our products are available in bookstores everywhere.

www.newworldlibrary.com

At NewWorldLibrary.com you can download our catalog,
subscribe to our e-newsletter, read our blog,
and link to authors' websites, videos, and podcasts.

Find us on Facebook, follow us on Twitter, and watch us on YouTube.

Send your questions and comments our way!
You make it possible for us to do what we love to do.

Phone: 415-884-2100 or 800-972-6657
Catalog requests: Ext. 10 | Orders: Ext. 52 | Fax: 415-884-2199
escort@newworldlibrary.com

NEW WORLD LIBRARY
publishing books that change lives   14 Pamaron Way, Novato, CA 94949